THE BUSH

THE PAST, THE PRESENT AND
THE FUTURE OF ALL THINGS RURAL

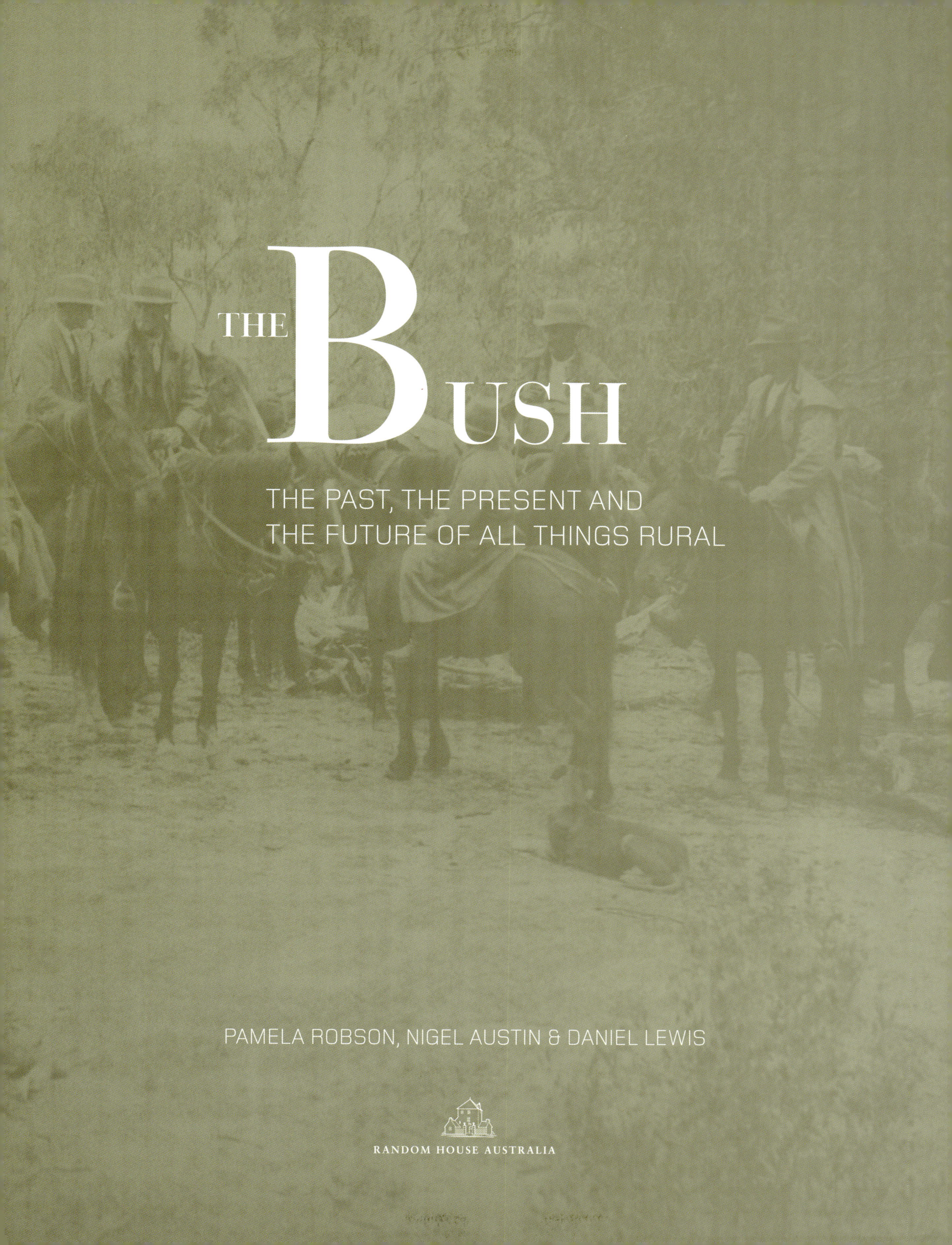

THE BUSH

THE PAST, THE PRESENT AND THE FUTURE OF ALL THINGS RURAL

PAMELA ROBSON, NIGEL AUSTIN & DANIEL LEWIS

RANDOM HOUSE AUSTRALIA

Contents

Foreword

Malcolm Turnbull

No matter how urban our surroundings, the Australian imagination is dominated by the bush.

Most of us live in the big cities on the coast—we are one of the most urbanised countries in the world. And yet, from the earliest times, the Australian bush and the people who live in it have formed an essential part of the image of our nation.

Back in the early 19th century, British writers extolled Australia as a rural paradise—an Arcady in utopia—in their efforts to promote immigration. And then there were the bush poets, such as A.B. 'Banjo' Paterson, who ensured that the archetypal Aussie was not the city worker, but the lean, laconic stockman.

Paterson was a city solicitor and yet he wrote our most memorable bush verse. 'Waltzing Matilda' is our most beloved national song, and its hero is a sheep thief who drowns himself rather than be taken by the police. While the young horseman from the Snowy River is his most courageous character, Paterson's most romantic is the drover: 'Clancy of the Overflow'. Paterson battles in his "dingy little office" with the "round eternal of the cashbook and journal" and dreams of Clancy:

In my wild erratic fancy visions come to me of Clancy
Gone a-droving "down the Cooper" where the Western drovers go;
As the stock are slowly stringing, Clancy rides behind them singing,
For the drover's life has pleasures that the townsfolk never know.

And the bush hath friends to meet him, and their kindly voices greet him
In the murmur of the breezes and the river on its bars,
And he sees the vision splendid of the sunlit plains extended,
And at night the wond'rous glory of the everlasting stars.

City solicitors fantasise about the country life as much today as they did in Paterson's time. And, while much in the bush has changed with modern communications, much has also remained the same.

Earlier this year, as the drought devastated rural New South Wales, my own paddocks were bare of grass and I sent 350 head of cattle off with a drover along the travelling stock routes—the 'long paddock'—in the hope of finding something to eat. Today's drover has a caravan and a bike, and yet I am sure Clancy would feel very much at home as local authorities hurry the modern drover along lest, like Saltbush Bill, their stock linger too long and eat too much.

Of course, it was not just writers who brought the bush to life more than a century ago. The painters of the Heidelberg School, such as Frederick McCubbin, evoked the isolation, the dangers and, yes, the freedom and space of the bush for those of us living a cramped and secure existence in the cities.

This book celebrates the bush, its people, its history and its landscape. It reminds us, too, that despite the internet and television, life in the bush is unpredictable—we remain, as Dorothea Mackellar wrote, "the land of drought and flooding rains"; drought, in particular, continues to be as Henry Lawson penned, our "red marauder".

In these pages we learn the story of the original, often haphazard, encounters European settlers had with the bush. We are told the stories of men such as James Ruse, the former convict whose work at Experiment Farm would lead the way to the current sustainability, and Lieutenant John Macarthur, who was the first to hoist the Australian economy onto the sheep's back.

And we learn, too, about the Australian bush today—a world which is both romantic and real. The romance of the bush will always be part of what it is to be Australian. However, this book reminds us that the bush is a real place, of real people and real challenges: it is sustained by people upon whose shoulders sit the great export industries of agriculture and mining; the current drought has broken as many hearts as it has rainfall records, and the cost—both financial and emotional—has been immense.

The values that Australians admire are the values of the bush, born out of harsh conditions, isolation and a climate that is capriciously unreliable. Mateship, loyalty and a preparedness to take on any adversity; these values have served us well through good times and through bad.

The Australian Government has provided, and continues to provide, unprecedented amounts of support for rural Australians, from exceptional-circumstances income and interest support for those affected by drought to long-term programs such as the National Plan for Water Security to secure and sustain our rural water supplies.

This book reminds us, as if we could ever forget it, that the bush and those who live in it are at the very heart of Australia.

Malcolm Turnbull

Minister for Environment and Water Resources

September 2007

The sun sets behind an outback farmer watching over his land in far north NSW (photo: Quentin Jones).

The mystique of the bush

Daniel Lewis

Why do Australians have such a profound attachment to the bush? The answer to this question probably lies in the foundational experiences of some of the nation's earliest white settlers.

As the great French observer Alexis de Tocqueville once wrote:

> *The entire man is, so to speak, to be seen in the cradle of the child. The growth of nations presents something analogous to this; they all bear some marks of their origin; and the circumstances which accompanied their birth and contributed to their rise, affect the whole term of their being.*

When the Australian colonies formed a federation on January 1, 1901, the new country was a nation riding on the sheep's back.

Wool came from the bush and it shaped our early politics, economics, language, landscape, transport links and national self-image.

Sydney still accounted for less than half the population of NSW and it was the people of the bush—people who already identified themselves as Australians—who overwhelmingly supported the colonies becoming a nation. The frontier had a unifying, nationalist influence.

Russel Ward used de Tocqueville's quote to open *The Australian Legend*, first published in the 1950s and still regarded as one of the most important books about Australia.

Ward traced the historic origins and development of the 'national mystique' and found it was formed by the men of the pastoral frontier—drovers, bullock drivers and shearers—with characteristics "whose sum was comprised in the concept of mateship".

He argued that:

> *. . . a specifically Australian outlook grew up first and most clearly among the bush workers in the Australian pastoral industry, and that this group has had an influence completely disproportionate to its numerical and economic strength, on the attitudes of the whole Australian community.*

This nomad tribe of bush workers was a product of the unique outback environment it inhabited—a land of vast distances, temperature extremes, loneliness, unfamiliar flora and fauna, utterly foreign and sometimes hostile Aboriginal people, droughts, floods, dust storms and locusts.

In the burgeoning settlement, it was the pastoral and non-coastal frontier that was most different to the environment of Britain and therefore the place where people developed characteristics most different from those in the Mother Country. It was a place that created Australians, Ward said, because "life in a bark hut on the Bogan (River) necessarily changed the newcomers' manners and ideas more rapidly than life in a George Street (Sydney) cottage".

In the 1880s and 1890s, as Australia was marching towards nationhood, artists and writers latched onto this reality and romanticised it into the stereotypical national self-image that continues to exist today. Experiences and images of the bush inspired much of Australia's most revered early art and literature—poetry and writings by *The Bulletin*'s Banjo Paterson and Henry Lawson, and art from the Heidelberg school's Tom Roberts and Arthur Streeton.

The bushman effectively became the 1890s' version of the noble savage.

Ward's aim was:

> *. . . to trace and explain the development of the Australian self-image—of the often romanticised and exaggerated stereotype in men's minds of what the typical, not the average, Australian likes to believe he is like. The average Australian is necessarily much more like the average American.*

Bush poet Henry Lawson, at age 26 **(above left)**. Drovers, such as these men near Wagga Wagga during the 1951 drought **(above right)**, were true nomads; their enterprising spirit helped shape the nation's notion of 'Australians' (photo: Frank Burke). **Overleaf:** an evocative 1929 bush photo of Kuranda, Queensland, known to locals as 'Fairyland' (photo: H.H. Fishwick).

The 'typical' Australian male, Ward said, "will stick to his mates through thick and thin, even if he thinks they may be wrong."

The early poets and painters didn't just talk up the bush; they talked down the city.

In Paterson's 'Clancy of the Overflow', Clancy enjoys "the vision splendid of the sunlit plains extended, and at night the wondrous glory of the everlasting stars", while Paterson sits in his office amid "the fetid air and gritty of the dusty, dirty city" musing, "I somehow rather fancy that I'd like to change with Clancy".

In 1909, legendary journalist with *The Sydney Morning Herald*, Charles Bean, travelled the backblocks of NSW doing a series of reports on the wool industry.

Some years later, chronicling the legend of the Anzacs through his dispatches from Gallipoli, Bean wrote that those he had met in the bush:

> *. . . went to make up the men of Anzac . . . The traditions of the back country weighed far more heavily than the mere number of its representatives among the influences that moulded the Australian and New Zealand soldier.*

In his book, *On the Wool Track*, published in 1910, Bean mused that the people of the bush "must always be pioneers in many respects—and probably, therefore, a source of strength for their nation".

Of the outback, Bean added: "Out here you have reached the core of Australia—the real red Australia of the ages".

But for all the talk of 'the bush' and 'the outback'—the terms sometimes used interchangeably—a clear definition of where and what they are is not so readily available.

The bush lies somewhere beyond the McMansions, the lattes and the zinc cream of Australia's town and city fringes. It is the magnet that sees city people pack their cars to make a pilgrimage to some shimmering, far-away red dirt place or a cool riverbank campsite set among towering gum trees. It is the magic that makes Australians overseas yearn for golden wattle, impossibly vivid deep blue skies and the scent of eucalyptus. Its mystique drives the treechange phenomenon.

Identifying with the bush bolsters our masochistic Australian pride in defying the demons of droughts, floods, fires, storms, plagues and pestilence.

Many people in the bush these days bemoan what they call the city–country divide. For those in the eastern states the Great Dividing Range is now a "sandstone curtain" that physically and mentally separates the people of the bush from the people of the cities.

Despite widespread city-based sentimentalism for the bush, country people commonly feel their city cousins have forgotten them, believing that the genuine affection urban people once had for them is gone. The claim that city people think milk comes from a cardboard carton is a common country refrain.

There is some truth in all of this: increasingly, city people are ignorant of country ways. Migration is another significant factor, with Australia's city populations hailing from global rather than British backgrounds. The prevailing and often rich and recent rural heritage among many Australians now is Asian, Middle Eastern or Mediterranean, far removed from the uniquely Australian rural culture which has adapted over two centuries to vast distances and extremes of environment and climate.

Certainly, Australian city folk continue to demonstrate an abiding (albeit idealised) interest in rural and country life in their support for bush-based films, TV shows and magazines. And every year, each state capital holds its royal show: a grand version of the many smaller country shows. The bush comes to town and the people of the town come to see the parades and exhibits. They devour the rides and the showbags, but they also pay a visit to the regional produce displays, the cattle pavilion, the rodeo, the petting farm, the shearing demonstrations and the woodchopping. They buy tea and delicious scones with jam and cream at the Country Women's Association canteen. And they sit for hours watching livestock parades and judging in the main arena. It's country, and they love it.

'Advance Australia Fair' is our turgid national anthem, but most Australians would rather have 'Waltzing Matilda'—Banjo Paterson's tale of a sheep-thieving swagman inspired by the true story of a bloody shearers' strike. We love the flying kangaroo of Qantas because the 'Spirit of Australia' symbolises the airline's birth in the outback

Queensland town of Longreach. The bush visits us all whether it be via advertising logos and food or images of bushfires and dust storms.

As John Thornhill wrote in his book, *Making Australia*:

> *Being Australian involves coming to terms at a very fundamental level with the physical environment of our continent. Human existence and identity, whether personal, political or cultural, is of its nature realised in and through relationships to a particular society and to the physical environment which shapes its culture.*

When you live in Dorothea Mackellar's sunburnt country, the bush is still as Australian as sunburn and just as likely to leave its mark on all of us. It may be that we no longer all have an aunt or a cousin living on the land, but in the 21st century our attachment to the institution of the bush is still strong.

When R. M. Williams died in 2003 aged 95, the old outback bootmaker who founded a bush-based fashion and equipment empire was honoured with an outpouring of emotion and a state funeral.

Just a few months earlier the nation stopped to pay its respects to country singer and musician Slim Dusty. The send-off was more than a state funeral. Across the land, Australians watched, knowing it was the end of an era; the close of a great chapter in the shaping of their identity.

It was the day an unassuming country musician officially joined Lawson and Paterson in the realm of legend. Sydney's St Andrew's Cathedral became a hand-clapping hillbilly heaven and a minister many call a wowser led the singing of 'A Pub With No Beer'. There could be no greater symbol of the influence of Slim Dusty than the fact that the congregation of St Andrew's, from the Prime Minister to the pall bearers, sang as one:

> *Oh it's a-lonesome away from your kindred and all*
> *By the campfire at night we'll hear the wild dingos call*
> *But there's nothing so lonesome, morbid or drear*
> *Than to stand in the bar of a pub with no beer.*

Australian bush legend, R.M. Williams, who turned an outback bootmaking business into an internationally recognised fashion empire. He was honoured with a state funeral when he died, aged 95, in 2003.

From outback truck stops to isolated Aboriginal settlements to the packed pavements of George Street, people paused to sing along and pay their respects to the man who had honoured the bush and helped keep millions of urban Australians in touch with it.

He was laid to rest in a coffin draped in the Australian flag and topped with a battered Akubra, its brim bent at that familiar angle.

The Dean of St Andrew's, Phillip Jensen, said Slim had some things in common with Jesus Christ. "Both were rural storytellers travelling from town to town to little villages amongst the ordinary people . . . telling their stories, encountering life as it is," he said.

And while Jesus might not have had a good pub yarn about beer—"the ordinary bloke's drink"—he could do a mean party trick turning water into wine.

"'A Pub With No Beer' is about mateship, the friendship of drinking together as equals contrasted with the misery of loneliness," Dr Jensen said. "The drinking of beer is symbolic of enjoying mateship. We have lost a mate and it is a sad day for the whole nation."

Slim's family, friends and legion of fans farewelled him as he had famously farewelled them at the end of each show: "Goodbye, God bless and many happy campfires".

When drought started to bite in 2002, some of Australia's wealthiest and most influential figures—the late Kerry Packer, Alan Jones, Bob Mansfield, Richard Pratt, John Singleton—started the Farmhand Appeal which raised tens of millions of dollars to assist struggling farmers.

And when drought again savaged much of Australia in 2006, some scientists and environmentalists said there were areas that simply couldn't sustain agriculture and that farmers should be paid to leave rather than receive a fortune in government drought assistance.

But the Prime Minister was having none of it. "We must maintain our faith as a nation in the farming community," John Howard said.

> *We would lose something of our identity as a nation, an important part of our psyche as a nation, if our rural communities fell below a critical mass. The essence of being an Australian includes the bush being part of our existence.*

The Opposition didn't quibble.

One of Australia's most famous outback towns, Bourke, sits in the midst of hard country regularly plagued by drought. Some say it is too marginal and that white Australians should have heeded the words of explorer Charles Sturt who in 1829 declared it was a place that would "never be the haunt of civilised man".

But as Henry Lawson once famously remarked to a friend: "If you know Bourke you know Australia".

The vast majority of Australians will never visit the struggling outback town on the banks of the Darling River in north-west NSW—but they know what Lawson meant. They know that being Australian is intrinsically linked to life in the bush.

Some urban Australians may have come no closer to the bush than a Slim Dusty song, a Henry Lawson poem or a bowl of wattleseed ice-cream, but many have savoured at least some of its countless sweet and sour offerings.

They treasure memories of sitting around a campfire yarning to mates on the banks of the Darling River; standing beer in hand at the finishing post of the Louth races as the horses pound past in a cloud of dust; watching shearers sweat it out in the oven of a corrugated iron woolshed on Eureka Plains station near Enngonia; punting on the yabby races at Windorah; watching the bulls win at the Yass rodeo.

Those who have spent time in the bush know that they must leave gates as they find them, and they'll know to close the gate behind them on the dog fence that runs along the NSW–Queensland border when they enter the village of Hungerford.

The Royal Flying Doctor Service brings a warm glow to the hearts of most Australians, especially those who have experienced first-hand the reassuring thrum of a life-saving aircraft coming in to land on a dirt runway hundreds or thousands of kilometres from the nearest town.

From choking on the smoke as a fire storm races through the Blue Mountains to spotting a koala in the Pilliga Scrub, it is these kinds of magic moments—and millions more like them—that sustain the enduring mystique of the Australian bush.

The Royal Flying Doctor Service has made rural Australia a safer place to live, and is a symbol of the triumph of initiative and courage over adversity. Here, station hands help the pilot to refuel the aircraft for its flight to Broken Hill, in 1950 (photo: Len Drummond).

This image of a group of Western Australian farm workers captures our culture of camaraderie.

The settling of Australia

Nigel Austin

James Ruse began harvesting the first successful wheat crop grown in the colony of New South Wales in a clearing near Rose Hill on a spring morning in 1789. Tirelessly, the wiry sun-bronzed man reaped this first small crop and bound it into sheaves. As the sun rose higher into the sky, the stacks awaiting threshing grew steadily larger.

By the time ex-convict James Ruse had completed this first successful harvest, news of the momentous event had reached Governor Arthur Phillip, 16 miles (almost 26 kilometres) east at the struggling convict town of Sydney. Twenty-two months after the First Fleet landed at Port Jackson, Ruse's harvest was greeted with great excitement by the food-hungry penal colony. Governor Phillip, who had personally entrusted Ruse with the first private farm in NSW and the vital task of producing grain for the colony, was particularly encouraged.

The governor had ordered in November 1788 that:

> *. . . a hut be built in a good situation, an acre* (0.4 hectares) *of ground cleared, and once turned up it was* (to be) *put into the possession of a very industrious convict, who was told if he behaved well he should have 30 acres* (just over 12 hectares).

That convict was Ruse, who had decided when his sentence expired in August 1789 that his future lay in NSW rather than in returning to England. Although the yield from Ruse's 1.5 acre (0.6 hectare) harvest was insufficient to provide more than seed for the next season's planting, it was enough to offer hope that the colony would one day become self-sufficient in food.

When his second crop was also successful, Ruse was rewarded with a 30 acre grant, two sow pigs and six hens at Rose Hill in April 1791. This, the first land grant in Australia, was named Experiment Farm. Ruse's farming background in Cornwall—he was born in a tiny thatched cottage near Launceston in 1760—gave him the knowledge to succeed on his little farm. In his own words, he was "bred a husbandman", working on the land from an early age, so that when he arrived in NSW, he was one of the few with any practical farming experience.

Ruse related the story of his early success to Watkin Tench who published it in *A Complete Account of the Settlement of New South Wales*, in 1793:

> *I have now an acre and a half in bearded wheat, half an acre in maize, and a small kitchen garden. On my wheat land I sowed three bushels of seed, the produce of this country, broad cast. I expect to reap about 12 or 13 bushels. I know nothing of the cultivation of maize, and cannot therefore guess so well at what I am likely to gather . . .*
>
> *My land I prepared thus: having burnt the fallen timber off the ground, I dug in the ashes, and then hoed it up, never doing more than eight, or perhaps nine, rods in a day, by which means, it was not like the Government farm, just scratched over, but properly done; then I clod-moulded it, and dug in the grass and weeds: this I think almost equal to ploughing. I then let it lie as long as I could, exposed to air and sun; and just before I sowed my seed, turned it all up fresh. When I shall have reaped my crop, I propose to hoe it again, and harrow it fine, and then sow it with turnip-seed, which will mellow and prepare it for next year.*
>
> *My straw, I mean to bury in pits, and throw in with it every thing which I think will rot and turn to manure. I have no person to help me, at present, but my wife, whom I married in this country, she is industrious . . . My opinion of the soil of my farm, is that it is middling, neither good nor bad. I will be bound to make it do with the aid of manure, but without cattle it will fail. The greatest check upon me is the dishonesty of the convicts, who, in spite of all my vigilance, rob me almost every night.*

This humble but vital start for Australian agriculture provided few clues that the new country would, one day, become one of the world's great agricultural nations. No one could have foreseen the growth of this industry in the next 200 years.

From the very beginning, the new settlers arriving in Australia were intent upon agricultural development, if only to ensure their survival. When the First Fleet arrived at Sydney Cove in Port Jackson on January 26, 1788, it carried aboard its 11 ships a collection of domestic animals which included 46 sheep, 28 pigs, eight cattle, seven horses, four goats and various poultry and rabbits from Cape Town in South Africa.

The early British settlers thought this vast ancient landscape of 768,230,000 hectares, with its apparently large areas of first-class grazing and cropping land, had all the right attributes for sustainable development. All it needed was men with will and character to establish a new civilisation far from the rest of the world. From the start, distance was its great bugbear: distance from markets, distance from the world, distance from one centre of civilisation in Australia to another.

Few countries began under more trying conditions. Governor Phillip wrote to Lord Sydney on May 15, 1788:

> *The great labour in clearing the ground will not permit more than eight acres* (3.2 hectares) *to be sown this year with wheat and barley. At the same time the immense number of ants and field-mice will render our crops very uncertain.*

Again in July, Phillip lamented:

> *The greatest part of the stock brought from the Cape is dead, and from the inattention of the men who had the care of the cattle, those belonging to Government and two cows belonging to myself are lost. As they have been missing three weeks, it is probable they are killed by the natives. All my sheep are dead, and a few only remain of those purchased for Government. The loss of four cows and two bulls falls very heavy. The horses do very well.*

The white population of the burgeoning colony was heavily weighted towards males. For many years from the arrival of the First Fleet, men greatly outnumbered women. The ships left England with 565 men, 192 women and 18 children; 32 convicts died during the long journey. Within a few months of landing, Governor Phillip was lamenting "the very small proportion of females" in the new country.

The authorities initially held few fears about the indigenous inhabitants, wrongly believing they were small in number and would pose little threat. Botanist Joseph Banks, during his voyage to the South Seas with Captain James Cook in 1770, saw very few Aborigines. He did not think there were more than 50 in all the Botany Bay area, and had reason to believe the country was very thinly peopled.

After arriving at Botany Bay, Governor Phillip was determined to remain at peace with the Aboriginal people. But despite his best intentions, misunderstandings led to a series of incidents and before the turn of the century, increasing skirmishes were occurring between the new settlers and the local Aboriginal population. The convicts collected animals and gum to sell to people on board the ships, and also built up a flourishing trade in spears, shields and other articles taken from the Aborigines. Ill feeling grew as it became clear that these implements were often the only means for the Aboriginal people of obtaining their daily food.

As the Aboriginal inhabitants and white settlers grew more familiar with each other, the incidents became more serious, leading eventually to deaths on both sides.

The land was increasingly turned to the purposes of the new inhabitants, but the rights of the existing occupiers, the Aborigines, were not covered by any treaty or agreement. Indeed, their knowledge of the land was put to little use by the newcomers with their English ideas about farming.

Soon houses, villages, churches and other buildings rose from the wilderness. Tracks wound their way through the new colony, trees were chopped down, and the land was slowly opened up for productive use.

By February 1790, Experiment Farm at Rose Hill had a barn, a granary and other necessary buildings. A good crop was also in the offing with 77 acres (31 hectares) of corn

BLACKS VISITING OUT-STATIONS.

The cartoonist's view of the turbulent relationship between indigenous Australians and the first settlers: 'Blacks visiting out-stations' **(above left)**, where a settler barters with Aborigines for artefacts; 'First Fleet and the Aborigines' **(above right)**, by the Walkley Award-winning illustrator John Spooner.

planted. Rose Hill had become the centre of agricultural operations and by the end of 1791, 31 emancipists (including Ruse) and three convicts were farming privately in the district on blocks of between 30 and 50 acres (12 and 20 hectares). Ground in cultivation at Parramatta included 351 acres (142 hectares) of maize, 44 acres (18 hectares) of wheat, six acres (2.4 hectares) of barley, one acre (0.4 hectares) of oats, two acres (0.8 hectares) of potatoes and various other land cleared for planting with crops, vegetables or for feeding livestock.

James Ruse and his wife Elizabeth, also an emancipated convict with a country background, suffered the first of many setbacks in 1793 when a disastrous harvest forced the sale of Experiment Farm for 40 pounds (about $100) to Surgeon John Harris, later to become one of the first directors of the Bank of NSW. Experiment Farm Cottage, built by Harris, remains on the site of the original farm and in 1963 was gifted to the National Trust of Australia in a ceremony at which Sir Eric Woodward, the Governor of NSW, officiated.

The colony's next growth phase occurred a little further west of Sydney town along the Hawkesbury River in early 1794 with the intrepid and determined Ruse one of the first to take up a grant. Ruse settled on 30 acres (12 hectares) at the junction of the Hawkesbury and Ruse's Creek (later known as South Creek), little realising the threat facing his land from constant floods, despite warnings from the Aborigines and ample evidence in trees along the river. Hard on the heels of Ruse came another 20 settlers, each granted 30 acres near where Windsor now stands. So rich was the soil that this number had grown to 400 settlers by June 1795, with farms stretching along both banks of the river for more than 30 miles (48 kilometres). The early wheat crops yielded between 30 and 36 bushels an acre, quickly making the Hawkesbury district the most important farmland in the colony.

In November 1795, the colony received some rare good news when the riddle of the missing cattle (the ones that had wandered off shortly after the arrival of the First Fleet) was solved. Five cows, two bulls and about 40 of their descendants were discovered south of Parramatta on the other side of the Nepean River in country that became known as the Cowpastures.

It was a significant discovery at the time, but it was not until the Blue Mountains were crossed in 1813 that sufficient land was available to seriously expand the flocks of sheep and herds of cattle. For instead of the grassy plains of which Sir Joseph Banks had spoken, the colonists encountered a heavily timbered coastal plain enclosed by an impassable mountain range.

From the beginning of settlement, a series of strange notions had grown about the mysterious land beyond the mountains. It was variously seen as a desert scorched by winds as devastating as the 'Khamseen of Egypt', a great pastoral plain, a Utopia for white people and an easy escape route to China for the convicts. Many men perished trying to 'escape' from the penal settlement of NSW before the path through the mountains was found.

A few years after the Cowpastures discovery, Governor Hunter heard a rumour that a group of convicts was planning a crude expedition several hundred kilometres to the south-west. In an attempt to dispel all the wild ideas, he decided to send out a party of explorers. The expedition was led by John Wilson, a former convict who had 'gone bush' after serving his sentence. Wilson had lived with the Aborigines for some time, dressing in kangaroo skins, etching his body with tribal markings and wearing his black hair long over his shoulders. He was accompanied on the expedition by four convicts, four soldiers and three bushmen. This party set out in January 1798 and while the convicts and soldiers soon tired of the rough country and returned to civilisation, Wilson and the bushmen went on.

They pushed on through the bush, further than any white man had travelled before in Australia. After a 26-day journey south-west through 400 kilometres of scrub to a point near the junction of the Wingecarribee and Wollondilly Rivers, Wilson and his men returned to Parramatta. A few weeks later, he set off once again with a larger party. This time they travelled for 560 kilometres to near the present site of Goulburn. Wilson then returned to his life in the bush and died in 1800, speared by an Aborigine while attempting to abduct a female member of the tribe.

The mystery of what lay beyond the Blue Mountains remained unsolved, despite countless official and unofficial attempts.

In 1789 Governor Phillip instituted a strong capitalist land grant system which had a significant impact on the early farming scene and a momentous long-term effect. Under this system, any officer who so desired was granted 100 acres (40 hectares) of land, along with 10 convicts to work it.

Lieutenant John Macarthur, profitably combining his private business activities with military duty, emerged as a principal figure in the colony's affairs at this time. In 1793, he began building a homestead on his property Elizabeth Farm at Rose Hill—a substantial sandstone cottage that more than 200 years later is the oldest European building in Australia. By late 1795, Macarthur had 50 cattle, 1000 sheep and a dozen horses, and was on his way to a place in history as the father of Australia's wool industry. He was also to become the first in the colony, in 1800, to use a plough which was drawn by either oxen or horse.

Despite Macarthur's success, by 1798 the general prosperity of farmers was poor; only 21 of Phillip's 73 settlers remained. A number had accepted land grants simply to sell out for a profit. The farming sector had already started to learn about the ongoing cycle of floods, droughts and bushfires.

When George Caley, a botanist, visited NSW in 1800, he wrote a series of disparaging reports to his patron Sir Joseph Banks before his departure in 1808:

> *The method of farming is conducted upon a bad principle, and is carried on in a slovenly manner. Nothing farther is done than to break up the ground with a hoe and throw in the wheat which again is chopped over with a hoe or harrowed. This is generally done in the months of March and April. The plough has been tried by some, but it does not seem to be preferred before the hoe. The stumps that yet remain in the ground are against it, and also the high price of cattle, but what appears to me to prevent its coming into frequent use is the want of workmen that know how to use it.*
>
> *I have never seen any people weed their wheat, though it is generally overrun with weeds, particularly a species of Lolium. The height of the harvest is about Christmas. The wheat is reaped in a slovenly manner, and a deal left scattered on the ground. After it is bound*

up into sheaves it is carried by men on their backs to the barn or stack. This is obliged to be done by those who have not horses or oxen which is chiefly the case throughout the colony . . . Such ways are not only attended with slowness and expense, but a great loss. When threshed it is but badly cleaned, and generally infested with oats or Lolium, particularly the latter, which is here called drake. In an English market it would fetch but an indifferent price.

The entrepreneurial Lieutenant John Macarthur (1767–1834), one of Australia's richest pastoralists. Macarthur's military, business and political activities dominated early colonial life while his efforts to develop a colonial export market pioneered Australia's wool industry.

The new settlement's land management patterns, such as over-cropping, have led to today's problems with salinity and erosion; this image shows land clearing in 1918, around Dairyville on the Upper Orara River, NSW.

Caley described the houses as in general:

> *. . . nothing more than simple wretched huts, particularly the farmers'. The walls are wattled, and plaistered with clay, the roof thatched, the floor frequently nothing more than the bare ground. They generally consist of two rooms, and the furniture coincides with them. The general mode of living is very mean and wretched, many have nothing but the store allowance, and those that are free, or off the stores, live nearly in the same manner.*

This early lacklustre approach towards farming and life in general by the ex-convicts set the pattern of land management that was to lead to problems in latter years. Over-cropping led to various kinds of land degradation including salinity, erosion and soil compaction that were to echo through the next 200 years of Australia's land settlement.

Nevertheless, by 1800 the colony was close to self-sufficiency in food with 138 horses, 709 cattle, 6003 sheep, 2763 goats, 3459 hogs, various other stock, 6125 acres (2480 hectares) of wheat and 2532 acres (1025 hectares) of maize.

At the end of its first 12 years the colony, known as the County of Cumberland, consisted of Sydney, Parramatta and 10 small farming settlements extending into the areas we now know as Camden, Emu Plains and the Windsor/Richmond district—an area of about 40 square miles (104 square kilometres). It had cost Britain more than one million pounds ($2.5 million). But for those with foresight, the first clue that this settlement might one day become a self-sustaining nation had come in 1797, with one of the most momentous events of the colony's first few decades. This was the importation of 13 Spanish merinos from the South African flocks of Colonel Gordon, the former Dutch Commander in Cape Town. These sheep ended up in the hands of John Macarthur, the Reverend Samuel Marsden and a handful of others.

While the First Fleet had brought about 70 fat-tails from South Africa and subsequent ships had arrived with various other breeds, particularly Bengal sheep from India, it was these first merinos that provided fine wool potential. Their introduction laid the foundations for an industry that was to carry the colony through its first 150 years to nationhood and economic stability.

John Macarthur, quick to take advantage of every opportunity, seized on this vision: that Australia's future lay in developing a wool industry. With plentiful land and convict labour, and the support of his gracious and accomplished wife, Elizabeth, his business undertakings thrived. An apparent setback—a pistol duel with his commanding officer in 1801—led to a court martial in England in early 1803. But following an acquittal, Macarthur used his remaining months in the Mother Country to promote Botany Bay as a future wool growing colony: at that time, by contrast with similar colonies, NSW lacked an important export commodity.

By fortunate circumstances and timing—for political reasons, Britain was in urgent need of increased wool supplies—Macarthur succeeded in persuading the British government to encourage fine wool growing in NSW. In 1803, he was already able to claim that he was the colony's largest sheep breeder and on this trip he exhibited the first samples of Botany Bay wool in England, while also enthusiastically promoting the development of a wool growing industry in NSW to the Lords of the Privy Council Committee on Trade and Foreign Plantations.

A statement by Macarthur to the Secretary of State for the Colonies read:

> *. . . that I have found, from an experience of many years, the climate of NSW peculiarly adapted to the increase of fine woolled sheep; and that, from the unlimited extent of luxuriant pastures with which that country abounds, millions of those valuable animals may be raised in a few years, with but little other expense than the hire of a few shepherds.*

The specimens that Macarthur had with him were inspected by the best judges of wool in the kingdom, who concluded that it was "equal in every valuable property" to the very best that was to be obtained from Spain. Macarthur gained approval to buy purebred merinos from the only flock in England, owned by King George III. Lord Camden, the Secretary of State, was so impressed by Macarthur's enterprise that he granted him 5000 acres (more than 2000 hectares) of the Cowpastures land by the Nepean River, and an ample supply of convict labour.

Elizabeth Farm, the Macarthur family estate: the 'Indian bungalow' design pre-empted the classic Australian homestead. Building commenced in 1793, and it once overlooked 1000 acres of agricultural land, stretching from Parramatta Road to the Parramatta River (photo: Steven Siewert).

In 1805, Macarthur returned in style to NSW with his merinos on his ship, the *Argo*. The first wool exported from Botany Bay to England sold at Garraway's Coffee House in 1807. But by 1809, Macarthur was again forced to leave the colony for his part in deposing Governor Bligh in the Rum Rebellion. He did not return until 1817: Macarthur, for all his guile, spent most of the period between 1800 and 1817 in exile.

During this time, his steadfast wife Elizabeth devoted herself to building up the Macarthur flocks and businesses. She ably managed the massive land holdings, the breeding programs and a convict labour force, communicating about marketing and sales by mail with her husband, while maintaining an exemplary and serene family home at Elizabeth

Farm. In fact, Elizabeth and her sons James and William are widely recognised as the steady, capable force that ensured the success often attributed solely to John Macarthur.

Between 1810 and 1820, as the Botany Bay name gained favour in Britain, the colony's flock trebled. Historically, this gestation period of the Australian wool industry was momentous, but the industry remained relatively unimportant until the 1820s due to the more immediate need for mutton. For the colony's first 50 years the whaling and sealing industries—'the fisheries', as they were known—were the main source of NSW's foreign trade and wealth.

Meanwhile, in 1798, James Ruse sold his first Hawkesbury land grant for 300 pounds ($750). It was a sound move; perhaps Ruse foresaw the hard times ahead. In March 1799, torrential rain ended a severe drought and the Hawkesbury River flooded, rising so quickly that the farms were submerged by a lake of water and a government storehouse was washed away. Many of the settlers were rescued from the roofs of their cottages by boat, but most of their personal belongings, small stock and facilities were washed away. The resulting loss of livestock and crops seriously affected the colony.

Ruse bought a cheap block of 20 acres (8 hectares) at Richmond Hill in 1800, but was forced to sell it after the Hawkesbury again flooded in 1801, on such a scale that he was once more nearly wiped out. This time the situation was so desperate that Ruse went to work as a seaman to keep his farmlands, leaving his wife Elizabeth to run the farms with convict labour.

The next major stage in Australia's development came in 1803 when Lieutenant-Colonel David Collins set off from England in command of two ships and 300 convicts to found a settlement at Port Phillip on the southern coast of the continent. But in early 1804, in direct contravention of his orders to settle and cultivate the land, Collins decided Port Phillip was unsuitable and moved the group to Sullivan Cove on the Derwent River at Hobart in Van Diemen's Land. (Lieutenant John Bowen had started a small outstation at Risdon Cove on the Derwent River in September 1803.)

These settlements, and another by Lieutenant-Colonel William Paterson at Port Dalrymple on the north coast of Van Diemen's Land in November 1804, were established after the discovery of a trade route through Bass Strait and amid fears that the French were about to settle southern Australia. At this time the 'fisheries' in southern Australia were booming. The records show that in 1802, 25,660 fur seal skins and 34 tons (31 tonnes) of elephant seal oil were sent to Sydney, for export mainly to China.

When Governor Philip Gidley King arrived in Sydney town in 1800, he realised the need for a new land policy and focused on emancipists, dispersing government herds and curtailing public agriculture. Under the new economic order, privately owned farms clearly prevailed over government farms. Wisely, King also decided that new industries such as wool "thrive so much better when conducted by the individual who has an interest in the produce".

From that time on, farming in the colony was left to private enterprise. The new policy provided plentiful encouragement for settlers of substance in the form of free convict labour for 18 months, large land grants and livestock.

The first free settler to take up the offer was Gregory Blaxland in 1806 followed in 1807 by his brother John, after selling their considerable Kent estates. The brothers, undoubtedly encouraged to emigrate by their friendship with Sir Joseph Banks, undertook to spend 6000 pounds ($15,000) on the 8000 acres (approximately 3250 hectares) they were granted. By 1805, the general muster in NSW showed there were 630 farm owners with 7000 acres (2850 hectares) of wheat, 5000 acres (2000 hectares) of maize, 1000 acres (405 hectares) of barley, 20,000 sheep, 20,000 hogs and 3500 goats.

The Ruses again suffered bad losses in subsequent floods, when the flooding of the Hawkesbury in 1809 plunged NSW into a state of near famine. The pattern of this family's fluctuating fortunes from floods, droughts, poor prices and recessions could have been a warning for any who followed on the land in the next 200 years. But eventually the Ruses' fortunes changed, helped by a 100 acre (40 hectare) grant at Salt Pan Creek on the George's River at Bankstown in 1809. Over the next few years, Ruse slowly built up his livestock of sheep, cattle, horses, pigs and poultry and also achieved his cherished ambition of owning a plough. Rather than buy one, the dogged Ruse built his own, a great heavy monstrosity that can be seen at the Powerhouse Museum in Sydney.

Ruse was either granted or owned 13 farms in his 40 years of farming and was one of the true pioneers of not just the farm sector but Australia. His wife Elizabeth died in 1836 and Ruse followed her 18 months later. He was buried beside her at Campbelltown where his self-inscribed tombstone reads:

Gloria in Axcelsis
Secred
to the memory
of James Ruse, who
departed this life
September 5, in the year of
houre Lord, 1837, Natef
of Cornwell, and arived
in this coleney by the
Forst Fleet, aged 77.
My Mother Reread Me tenderley
With Me She Took Much Paines
& When I Arived In This Coelney
I sowd the forst Grain and Now
With My Hevenly Father I hope
For Ever To Remain

In 2007, the quiet suburban Ruse Street in Harris Park marks the site of Experiment Farm which has been overtaken by houses and blocks of flats.

The real settlement of the Australian continent began with the momentous crossing of the Blue Mountains by Gregory Blaxland, Lieutenant William Lawson, William Charles Wentworth, and servants, in 1813. Blaxland, desperately in need of new land for his large

William Charles Wentworth **(above left)**, one of the first men to cross the Blue Mountains in search of more land. Lachlan Macquarie **(above right)**, governor of the new colony from 1810 to 1822 (photo: Robert Pearce, from the Lachlan Macquarie collection of rare books and manuscripts).

flocks of sheep and cattle, had decided that the answer was to find a route across the Blue Mountains. He was so moved by the important discovery that he declared they had found pastures to support the colony's livestock expansion for the next 30 years.

The crossing of the Blue Mountains (though not of the Great Dividing Range) certainly ended the colony's 25 years of confinement between the sea and a sandstone wall of mountains rising more than 900 metres in height. It extended NSW from a confined huddle stretching 130 kilometres north and south of Sydney and 65 kilometres inland, to a vast land almost the size of America.

Governor Lachlan Macquarie, after an inspection of the new country in 1815, was effusive in his praise. "Here was a land of fatness all untrod," wrote Macquarie. And: "There is abundance of as fine grazing land as any in the world within five or six miles (approximately eight or 10 kilometres) of Bathurst."

Already the vast continent was a place of opportunity; and the inland offered promise of a better life, the chance to rise and become a person of substance, something almost impossible to achieve in the old world.

Settlement until then had progressed rapidly with an increasing number of free settlers and a steady trickle of emancipists. By 1813, nearly 150,000 acres along the coastal strip was being farmed of which 85 per cent was pasture land.

The push westwards began slowly: by 1820 only 12 people had obtained permission to drove cattle across the mountains. But between 1821 and 1825 it rapidly gained momentum. In those few years, the number of people living outside the County of Cumberland rose from one per cent of the population to more than 10 per cent.

During this period, men still far outnumbered women in the colony. Those women who arrived in sound condition were often treated poorly, as is evident from a description in a *Report of the Select Committee of Transportation 1812*:

> *In the distribution of female convicts great abuses have formerly prevailed; they were indiscriminately given to such of the inhabitants as demanded them, and were in general received rather as prostitutes than as servants; and so far from being induced to reform*

An early lithograph illustrates the vices that infested the new colony: here, men and women, indigenous and European, enjoy a 'sly grog' shop at the Hanging Rock diggings.

themselves, the disgraceful manner in which they were disposed of, operated as an encouragement to general depravity of manners. Upon the arrival of Governor Bligh, two-thirds of the children annually born within the colony were illegitimate. Marriages have latterly become more frequent, consequently prostitution is stated to have been less prevalent; and Governor Macquarie is directing his endeavours, under order from the Government here, "to keep the female convicts separate till they can properly be distributed among the inhabitants, in such a manner as they may best derive the advantage of industry and good character."

At this time Governor Macquarie was arguing that the future of the colony depended on the arrival of more male convicts, while he regarded female convicts as a great drawback. But the Select Committee disagreed with him, admitting that while women were in many instances likely to "encourage the vices of the men, such women as these were the mothers of a great part of the inhabitants now existing in the colony".

At that time there were two men for every woman in the colony and as there were very few free settlers, there were even fewer women who were neither emancipist nor convict. By 1819 the disparity had grown even wider: there were 8920 male convicts and only 1066 female convicts, comprising 38.3 per cent of the total population of NSW.

Despite the shortcomings of Governor Macquarie's rule, he presided over an increase in cultivation and laid the foundations for the expansion of settlement. In his words:

> *... I found NSW a gaol, and left it a colony; I found Sydney a village and left it a city; I found a population of idle prisoners, paupers and paid officials, and left a large free community thriving in the produce of flocks and the labour of convicts.*

Macquarie's period saw considerable progress in all areas:

	1810	**1821**
Population	11,950	38,778
Cultivation (acres)	7615	32,267
Sheep	25,888	290,158
Cattle	12,442	102,939
Revenue (pounds)	8000	30,000

But even in these early years of the 19th century, few ploughs existed and most cultivation was carried out manually with simple hoes. An anonymous letter dated February 1819 gives a lucid account of the farming system:

> *The Farm is commenced by cutting down the Trees, leaving a Stump standing, from 2 to 3 Feet in height. The Butts and Heads of the Trees are then cut up, and packed together in large Parcels, and so burnt on the Ground. The Land so cleared, is generally a Spot chosen for the Soil being of good quality, and few Lands have been so cleared, but have produced good average crops, for the first 10 years, of about 20 Winchester Bushels of Wheat (weighing 60 Pounds to the Bushel) per English Acre.*
>
> *There is a tract of Hill Land, Prospect Hill which has been tilled upwards of 25 years without any Assistance of Manure of any Description, and still continues, in favourable seasons, to produce Average Crops as above stated—Many Farms of fine Hill Land have, however, been exhausted by this System of constant cropping and rendered totally useless. Many are now undergoing the dreadful Ordeal, and will soon be incapable of supporting their thoughtless possessors . . .*

The same writer lamented the lack of farm servants who understood the modern system of agriculture; and the want of good husbandry implements. He was especially critical of the lack of crop rotation and the continuous planting of crops with maize following wheat until the soil was exhausted. Yet if a rotational cropping system had been carried out, the wheat yields would have trebled from 10 bushels an acre to 30 bushels and the green rotation crop would have provided plentiful feed for livestock.

Nevertheless, for every setback, at least one step forward was made. The establishment of Australia's first bank came on April 8, 1817, when the Bank of NSW opened its doors in Sydney. It offered a badly needed service in providing credit, meeting the needs of business and in establishing a stable local currency. But even its early life was not without difficulty. The bank's special charter from Governor Macquarie for the incorporation of its president and directors as a limited liability company was without legal authority and did not receive official approval for another seven years. Today, as the Westpac Banking Corporation, it remains the oldest bank in Australia.

The next decade was a watershed in which the colonists struggled to come to terms with the new country. The first of the great explorers, Surveyor-General John Oxley, undertook two journeys in attempts to solve the riddle of the rivers, the Lachlan and the Macquarie. In 1817 Oxley travelled down the Lachlan to within 56 kilometres of the Murrumbidgee on his first trip, but was foiled by marshy ground and continued the speculation started a couple of years earlier by his surveyor George Evans that the rivers might flow into an inland sea in the centre of the continent. He travelled in a particularly wet season and also failed to appreciate the potential of the land.

On his 1818 trip down the Macquarie, Oxley was foiled by the Macquarie Marshes, and then travelled due east towards the coast. On this journey, the most substantial then undertaken in Australia, he discovered the Castlereagh River, the Liverpool Plains, the Peel River, the Hastings River and Port Macquarie and arrived at Port Stephens five months after leaving Bathurst.

Oxley was proclaimed a hero by the land-hungry colony for his discovery of rich new pastoral lands. But as always the problem was distance, and not for some time was a satisfactory direct path to the Liverpool Plains country found. This was in 1823 when Allan Cunningham, botanist to King George IV, found a break in the Liverpool Range which he named Pandora's Pass. Several years later Cunningham discovered a route north from the Liverpool Plains to some of the richest country in Australia, the Darling Downs.

The pastoralists became more important after the arrival in 1819 of John Thomas Bigge, commissioned to inquire into the colony's economy. Bigge, a London lawyer and formerly Chief Justice of the plantation colony of Trinidad, conducted his inquiry between 1819 and 1821 and his reports were prepared as parliamentary papers by the British Government in 1822–23. They covered general affairs, judicial establishments, agriculture and trade. Many of Bigge's recommendations were adopted by the British Government which was more interested in reducing costs than developing Australia as a strong, viable nation.

Bigge, like many of the wealthy free settlers into whose hands he fell, was prejudiced against the ex-convicts. His solutions lay in resurrecting public agriculture in convict settlements, processing wheat into by-products and building more granaries instead of addressing the more urgent need to seek export markets. Bigge recognised that the small settlers produced much of the grain in the colony, but believed their intensive production reduced the productivity of the land. He also believed their viability was reduced by the small size of their holdings, while the large pastoralists had far better prospects.

Consequently, Bigge recommended for emancipists:

> *... no grants of land exceeding 10 acres (4 hectares) in extent, or to those whose terms of sentence had expired, unless they could satisfactorily prove that they were possessed of capital amounting to no less than 20 per cent either in stock or implements ... The lower class of remitted convicts, and those whose terms of service are expired, will thus become resident labourers, rather than settlers, and their hope of future success will be more directed to their own industry and exertion, than to the early disposal and abuse of the indulgences of the Crown.*

After interviewing most free settlers in the colony, hundreds of convicts and about 50 emancipists, Bigge envisaged NSW becoming a vast sheep run employing thousands of convicts. He subscribed to the view of John Macarthur that the wool industry would provide a valuable and useful export commodity for trade with England and a profitable future for the settlers.

Meanwhile, pressures on land limitations were eased by Governor Brisbane when he opened up the Bathurst and Hunter Valley regions. Settlers flocked to the Hunter Valley and land on both sides of the river was soon occupied. By 1826, there were five settled areas in NSW: the Cumberland Plain around Sydney; the Bathurst district; the Hunter Valley; the Goulburn area; and the coastal plain around Illawarra.

Brisbane's term was also notable for events which paved the way for the settlement of what were to become the states of Queensland and Victoria. The first of these was the exploration of Moreton Bay and establishment of a penal colony in 1824. In the same year Hamilton Hume and W. H. Hovell travelled from Lake George in NSW to Port Phillip Bay. The year 1824 also marked the first attempted settlement of the Northern Territory with Captain Bremer sent to Melville Island.

By the mid 1820s three distinct groups of settlers made up the rural population in the colony. The first were the small farmers and emancipated convicts who were confined

Celebrations at Mamre Homestead, St Mary's, to mark the bicentenary of the first land grant to the Reverend Samuel Marsden, known as the 'flogging parson' for his tendency to order convict whippings (photo: Robert Pearce).

mainly to cropping. The second were the free settlers, normally men with capital and knowledge brought from mother England. The third group, the early colonists, included the first free settlers, wealthy Sydney merchants, former administrators and military men who arrived in the colony in its early days. This latter group were generally responsible for extending the outer limits of settlement, first by exploration and then by sending their herds and flocks in the care of stockmen. They included many of the important names of the colony: the Macarthurs, Blaxlands, Coxes, Samuel Marsden, Charles Throsby, Simeon Lord, John Wylde and Samuel Terry.

The phase of Australia's development from the 1820s onwards coincided with the emergence of a distinct national character and marked differences between Australian-born and British-born people. The two groups were sometimes referred to as Currency or Sterling, denoting colonial-born and English-born respectively. The names originated from a paymaster and referred to the difference in value between a pound currency and a pound sterling, the former holding less monetary value.

It perhaps had something to do with a superior diet in Australia, but the locally born—the Currency lads—were generally taller and were noted for their spirit, courage and clannishness.

The attraction of free land proved a great inducement to many settlers. At this time, while ex-convicts received only 30 acres (12 hectares) of land or slightly more, settlers with capital were given 2560 acres (1036 hectares), and sometimes several grants of this size. By 1831, 3,600,000 acres (1,456,868 hectares) of the best land in NSW and 2,057,000 acres (832,438 hectares) in Van Diemen's Land had been granted.

The administrators planned a system of agriculture based on that in England with yeoman farmers cultivating the land and forming the backbone of Australia, and large landholders who would rent out their land to small farmers. The largest land grant was one million acres (404,685 hectares) in 1824 to the Australian Agricultural Company, a Royal Charter company set up in London with capital of one million pounds (about $2,500,000) and backed by wealthy landowners including John Macarthur.

The migration of free settlers to NSW and Tasmania reached a substantial level for the first time in the 1820s when the first comprehensive accounts of Australia began appearing in England. Before then very few were willing to brave the voyage out or take the risk of settling in a new land. This period, from about the 1820s, set the scene for the nation's development for the next 150 years.

The lure of land was foremost, except for brief interludes when gold was king; rewards from land outshone those from gold, both individually and nationally.

Land-hungry seekers from all over the world came during this period including English landed gentry, Irish political refugees and Scottish settlers. Most had to adapt to an entirely new climate and country, unlike anything at home. The rainfall was inconsistent, and droughts and floods occurred at frequent intervals in the first 40 years. European methods were transplanted to Australia, but not until these were adapted to Australian conditions did the settlers achieve the success they desired.

Between 1825 and 1850, poverty in Great Britain drove three million people to the New World: Australia and New Zealand received 222,955 of them. North American colonies took 884,306 new settlers, the United States 1,750,682 and all other places 44,056. These people knew that land ownership meant wealth and power.

By 1846, there remained in the colony only 9563 male convicts and 912 women convicts, a mere 5.6 per cent of the NSW population. Social problems were prevalent, but the one great benefit these early settlers had was the healthy climate and relative freedom from a range of medical problems.

Throughout these early years much of the far-out land available for settlement remained unsurveyed. The surveying work that resulted in the establishment of the 'Nineteen Counties' (an area extending roughly to Kempsey in the north, Batemans Bay in the south and Wellington in the west) was left firstly to Oxley and then to Major Thomas Mitchell, the surveyor-general in NSW for 27 years.

To Mitchell goes much credit for his part in opening up the continent through his heroic exploration and surveying work. He is credited with the Great South and Great North Tracks leading from Sydney and an improved road across the Great Dividing Range. These three roads guided the development of the pastoral and agricultural industries for many years.

By the 1830s, NSW was on the verge of a dramatic escalation in pastoral settlement as men from the far corners of the world joined the land rush to the new colony. Land was the source of great fortunes, water the lifeblood, and cattle and sheep the conduit for turning grass into wealth.

The year 1831 marked the start of the second main period of land policy in the colony with the system of land grants—which had existed since 1788—being replaced by the Ripon regulations (named after the British Earl of Ripon). Under these regulations, the granting of crown land within the settled counties was replaced by auction sales with a minimum start-up price of five shillings. This was increased to 12 shillings in 1838 and a uniform fixed price of one pound an acre in the Port Phillip district was set in 1840.

Perhaps the shrewdest observations on the advancement of both NSW and the state of agriculture came in 1827 from Peter Cunningham in his book *Two Years in New South Wales*. They followed four journeys from England to Australia aboard convict ships as a surgeon for the Royal Navy. Cunningham warmly praised the:

> *. . . wonderful changes that have been wrought by the labour of the outcasts thrust by England from her bosom, to expiate their offences on these remote shores. It could scarcely have been conceived by the first founders that in transplanting a few incorrigible criminals into the wild woods of Australia, 16,000 miles (26,000 kilometres) distant from their native homes, the seeds of the mighty empire shown have been sown, which even at this day far exceeds, in rapidity of progress towards riches and power, any founded on the American continent.*
>
> *Those offenders have thus atoned to society by so valuable a legacy, good being produced from evil, and the native wilderness converted into an Eden . . . Where, 38 years ago, not a single European animal breathed, now upwards of 200,000 sheep and 100,000 head of cattle, and many thousand horses and other animals destined for the support and pleasure of man are peacefully grazing.*

As the herds of cattle and flocks of sheep increased in the 1820s and 1830s, their owners continued the search for new grazing lands. The pastoral settlement of large parts of the eastern and southern coastal fringes of Australia, including the south-west of Western Australia, began between 1825 and 1850 as the wealth promised by land ownership lured the pioneers in search of the best country.

Once NSW and Tasmania had been taken up, the third state to be settled was Western Australia. An exploratory party arrived in the Swan River district on Christmas Day 1826. After a good report, a permanent settlement started in 1829 when Captain Fremantle took possession of the western portion of Australia that was not included in NSW. The whole Australian continent thus formally became a Colony of the United Kingdom.

The colony of Van Diemen's Land, as Tasmania was then known, had been formally proclaimed in 1825. By 1830 much of the better land had been occupied and the colonists began to look across Bass Strait to Port Phillip Bay for new land. By the time Major Thomas Mitchell had journeyed from Sydney to western Victoria in 1836, the Henty family had been settled at Portland for two years.

Edward Henty, whose family owned one of the finest merino flocks in England, had arrived from Van Diemen's Land on November 19, 1834 to begin grazing livestock. The resourceful Henty was the first permanent settler in Victoria and the first to introduce sheep and cattle to the state, bringing them to his Portland property.

Mitchell's journey and the discovery of 'Australia Felix' were the catalyst for the rapid settlement of country in the Port Phillip district (renamed Victoria in 1851). A wealthy young Englishman, Joseph Hawdon, was the first man to overland cattle from NSW to Victoria in 1836, and between 1836 and 1838 a total of 5000 cattle were overlanded from the Canberra region to Melbourne. When the rich pasture lands of the Port Phillip district had been settled the next wave of settlers looked west to South Australia where farms had been established in 1836.

Further impetus for the settlement of the inland and South Australia had come in 1828 when Captain Charles Sturt discovered the Darling River and the following year traced the Murray River to its mouth on the South Australian coastline. Sturt's glowing report of the country between Lake Alexandrina and St Vincent's Gulf hastened the settlement of South Australia. Its development started with a rush as 15 ships arrived between July and December 1836. The country proved good grazing land and the overlanders, led by Joseph Hawdon and Charles Bonney in 1838, soon arrived with stock from the Port Phillip and Sydney districts. They were followed 12 weeks later by Edward John Eyre.

The South Australian Company, run by the Angas family, quickly proved an influence and by the end of 1838 had settled 19 farmers on small farms. The number grew rapidly and by 1839 a total of 41 farmers were renting land from the company.

The settlement of Queensland was left to last for although the potential of the Darling Downs in southern Queensland was discovered in 1827, the arrival of the first settlers was to take another 13 years. Allan Cunningham had left Segenhoe station in the Hunter Valley and briefly explored the region in 1827 before returning home. The following year he travelled by ship to Moreton Bay and then overland to the country he had explored the previous year. Slowly the settlers moved north from Sydney taking up new land towards the Queensland border, but the Darling Downs remained unsettled until 1840 when Patrick Leslie arrived. This quickly opened the way for others and indeed for the settlement of Queensland. After the initial settlements the pioneers quickly pushed on through the Queensland hinterland in a multitude of directions as they sought new land.

By the 1850s, a significant part of Australia had been settled, leaving northern Australia as the last frontier. Its time came from the 1860s onwards as the frontiersmen from Queensland and the southern states trickled into the northern regions, exploring as they travelled and dreaming of fortune and glory by selecting good land at low crown rentals.

It was to be many years before the north was to reach its potential.

From these humble beginnings and difficult early years, the Australian nation was born with its own distinctive character. One endearing characteristic, from as early as 1801, was the description of the countryside beyond the cities as 'the bush' after the Dutch word *bosch*. Borrowed from the Cape of Good Hope, the term quickly replaced English words such as 'woods' and 'forest'.

Other unique characteristics swiftly developed, in keeping with the rapid evolution of a new society in those early days, and established the foundations of a new way of life for the many people who poured into the Australian colonies in the following decades.

Dust swirls as Brahman steer are mustered on Brunette Downs cattle station, NT (photo: Brendan Esposito).

Life in the remote outback

Pamela Robson

The full moon that hangs over the vast silent spaces of Australia's interior seems brighter and more luminous than any other. Its silvery sheen can turn night into ghostly day. Visitors remark on it. Tourist operators run outback safaris to coincide with it. It has traditionally been the 'clock' that sets the calendar for remote Aboriginal communities. It lights the stage for corroborees, ceremonies, hunting and catching fish, and in earlier days, the settling of old scores. Full moon is also the time when the giant cattle stations of the northern interior can extend the working day to muster the big herds of Brahman before moving them south and east.

Here, thousands of kilometres from the nearest city or street light (think New York to Moscow or London to Istanbul) everything depends on the natural world and runs to a different sort of clock. Forget nine to five—out here, it's dawn till dusk. This is the closest you'll get to the middle of nowhere. There are no lights, no people, no cars, no sounds—just ceaseless space and deafening silence. The immensity takes your breath away.

Clinging to the coastal strip that rims the continent, most of us have little idea of what it's like to live in the huge expanse that is the middle of Australia. The nearest we get is via an airliner window where, from the comfortable altitude of 11,000 metres, we can watch the scorched red earth and the tiny dots of remote settlements silently slide by.

Australia is one of the most urbanised countries in the world. About 85 per cent of Australians live in the cities and suburbs. And only a small percentage of urban dwellers have ventured beyond the residential acreage belt and into the bush. This means there are two quite separate Australias existing side by side, sharing the same continent. And with every decade they seem to slip further apart.

To borrow from novelist L. P. Hartley—the outback is foreign country; they do things differently there. And why wouldn't they? In such a physically hostile environment, each community has to be self-sufficient, because there is no one close by to offer support or assistance. It helps to be physically capable, mechanically handy and able to fix things, and, most importantly, mentally resilient.

You might have a PhD in mathematics, be able to do *The Sydney Morning Herald* cryptic crossword on the run, or manage a global corporation, but out here, it counts for nothing if you can't change a tyre on the Toyota, open a bush gate from the back of a horse, fix the generator, or remove a king brown snake from under the laundry. The people who live in the remotest parts of Australia know better than most that you have to take the rough with the smooth if you want to get the best out of life.

Until very recently, communications with the outside world have been infrequent and they can still be unreliable. Travelling is often hazardous. This is the country where, to the untutored eye, there are no definable landmarks. Roads—even unsurfaced tracks—are few and light aircraft is generally the way to go.

During the wet season, which affects the northern parts of Queensland, the Northern Territory and Western Australia, the flood waters can stretch for hundreds of kilometres and last for weeks on end. This is the time when nature is at her most powerful, when lightning bolts of awesome force illuminate the sky every afternoon, and when summer cyclones obliterate the landscape.

This is when the thermometer can soar to a sweltering 50 degrees Celsius and the humidity reaches saturation point. The cyclones start just after Christmas, often coming in at night and bringing a blackness like no other. Dense cloud formations roll along low to the ground and stretch 16 kilometres into the sky. Wind gusts of 180 kilometres or more slice off rooftops and raze entire buildings to dust.

Settlements and cattle stations that were once reachable in 'a day on dirt' are isolated by water. During the wet, they can be as remote as any Antarctic field base. For months on end, there is no movement in or out except by air—this is when light aircraft become the lifeline.

If you want to live in the outback, you have to be able to deal with the isolation. And this is not a skill with which the modern world equips us. Google the word 'remote' into the computer and up flashes a list of companies wanting to sell a control for the TV. Tap in 'isolation' and you'll get a series of empathetic sites aimed at solving the problems of living alone in the city.

Yet the outback is full of people who are happy to be there, who like the quiet and relish the solitude, and who get nervous when they see a street light.

The inland population is made up of people in small townships, mining communities, Aboriginal communities and on cattle stations. Australia's northern cattle stations are some of the largest in the world. Many cover thousands of square kilometres and are the size of small European countries, yet even the biggest have resident populations that are usually less than 20.

Arriving at a big cattle station, you will most likely see a cluster of neat timber buildings set around a bright green patchwork of well-kept gardens with established trees for shade. There will usually be an airstrip and a few big sheds. Surrounding them in all directions will be the endless stretches of Mitchell or Flinders grasses with varying densities of Spinifex scrub depending on which type of country you are in.

Out here, in the back of beyond, routine is everything. The working day starts with breakfast just before dawn, then there's smoko at 9.30, lunch at 12.30 and dinner at 7pm. The best place to meet people is in the big kitchen at meal times. This is the heart of station life.

Typically, the community on a big station is made up of the owner or manager, his wife and family, the assistant manager and family, and the station hands—ringers, jillaroos and jackaroos. There's often the boreman and the plant drivers. On the big stations there are pilots—usually dually licensed for fixed wing and helicopters. When a station is family-owned, there is always at least one person who can fly a plane. They act as high-altitude chauffeurs, taking people to town, bringing in provisions and standing by in case of emergencies. Importantly, they have the special skills needed to muster cattle by helicopter.

When there are children on a station, there will probably be a governess. And there is always the cook. The cook, as everyone will tell you, is the most important person in the small community. It is common for wives to work on the station—either in the office, in the kitchen, or in the yards alongside the men. Then there are the visitors—cattle buyers, vets, mechanics, and so on. Ask any manager's wife and she will tell you that running a big station can be a bit like running a hotel. Food is ordered and bought in bulk. The larger stations often have a big cool room where everything that doesn't come in tins or cartons can be stored.

It's still dark when the station hands pull on their jeans, shirts and boots and head off for breakfast. And it's always a big breakfast of steak, sausages, rissoles, eggs, tomatoes and beans. They'll need every calorie. They'll be hard at work until well after dusk.

Although technology and science have changed the way cattle are managed, the work is as physically demanding as ever. It's hard; and at times it's dangerous. Most of the action revolves around mustering the cattle from the big paddocks, or working on them in the yards. It's pretty much year round—from calving in the summer months, to pregnancy testing, branding, and weaning and then, ultimately, manoeuvring them into the big road trains and off to the feedlot or meatworks.

Most of the work is carried out on horseback. Australia is one of the few countries in the world where horses are still in genuine work, and there's a good reason why. There's a saying on the stations: quiet cattle are fat cattle. And fat cattle produce the best quality meat. The whole focus of animal management is to keep the herd stress free. Although the Australian cattle industry flirted with motorised mustering for a while, it didn't take long to realise that helicopters and motorbikes caused too much bovine tension and so it was back to the traditional way on horseback. Typically nowadays, helicopters or light aircraft round up the animals from the outlying areas and guide them towards the stockmen and women on horseback who walk them quietly all the way to the holding yards.

Each station hand has a string of about two or three horses which are rotated, with one in work and the others resting. In the old days, a stockman could have had as many as

The masterful head stockmen from Anna Creek cattle station, the largest in the world; this photograph was taken in September 1997 (photo: Steven Siewert).

eight or nine horses. But thanks to better horse management and nutrition, station horses these days are generally healthier and in better condition and need fewer rest periods.

The Australian stockhorse is the preferred breed—sometimes crossed with thoroughbred blood for speed, Arabian for endurance or American quarter horse for athleticism and the ability to turn on the haunches.

The best horses have a temperament that is quiet, manageable and safe, so they can be ridden and worked without drama by just about anybody. They have to be fast, sure-footed, and have good eyesight at night. The best are station bred which means they have the added benefit of being more sure-footed—they know the terrain. And this has real safety advantages. Just watch a group of foals cavorting around in a paddock and you'll wonder how they survive without breaking a leg. They soon learn to instinctively negotiate loose rocks, unseen holes and hidden tree roots.

The pride taken by stockmen and women in developing their horse management skills and making a name for themselves across the full range of activities such as breaking in, handling colts, shoeing and, of course, riding, has created a potent culture in the pastoral industry. Strong bonds develop between riders and their horses. Fond memories of a horse can last a lifetime, while some horses are best forgotten. Even the toughest blokes will admit to occasionally staying awake most of the night worrying about a difficult or unpredictable horse they have to ride the next day. These are the tough guys who don't mind a fight in the pub—but the thought of a bucking horse at first light over rough ground does not bode well for a good night's sleep.

Put any group of bush people together regardless of age and it is a safe bet that horsemanship in some form or another will come into the conversation. Ask anyone on the stations why they are there and their answer is sure to include something about horses. Everyone you talk to is passionate about them. They're central to the lifestyle and play a huge role in attracting new people and in keeping them there. Social life revolves around them whether it's horse racing, polocrosse or that most beloved of Australian sports, campdrafting.

Whereas once it was a given that the family farm would be handed down through the generations, increasingly the country's youth—such as this young boy pictured in June 2001—say they have no ambition to follow in their parents' footsteps (photo: Pat Scala).

At a time when fewer young people are staying on the land, preferring the wider options offered by the city or the big pay packets of the mining companies, those who stay on the stations generally do so for the lifestyle. They'll tell you that the dust, flies and heat are worth enduring for the unique experiences.

In the old days, tradition dictated that the eldest son would inherit the family property, but increasingly families want to see as many of their children go on to tertiary education as can be mustered. These days, it's not uncommon to find that the owner of a cattle station has done a business or law degree. Equally, a younger son or daughter might be the one who takes on the job of running the family farm when dad dies. All too frequently, properties are sold because no one in the family wants to take on the tough work and the long, hard days, or have the worry of the bank balance in times of drought. Many on the land are asset rich but exist on small incomes.

Traditionally, the large majority of properties in Australia have been family businesses. But since the 1950s, the introduction of new technologies, the globalisation of commodity markets, and the removal of tariffs have changed the landscape. As a rule of thumb, larger properties are more economically viable than smaller ones. Throughout the 1970s

More women are training to be jillaroos, aiming for a career mustering cattle on stations. Jillaroos are considered by many to be the industry's most talented and capable horse handlers (photo: Glenn Campbell).

and 1980s there was a gradual restructuring of the rural sector as more corporations were established and entered the pastoral industry. Multiple properties were acquired and amalgamated and when they were next sold, they were often auctioned as a group. This meant they were usually priced out of the reach of most families. It became less easy for the family to compete. Many families trying to make a living off the land found that their income was being reduced over time and in many cases at least one member—usually the wife—has been forced to work off-farm to supplement the household income.

Increasingly, the labour force is being drawn from young people outside the bush who don't have any experience in cattle and are attracted as much as anything by the adventure. There are also more young women coming into the industry. Once, they came as governesses or nurses. Now, they work alongside the men in the yards and out in the paddocks. On some stations, they out-number the men.

Cattle stations were one of the last all-male workplaces in Australia. But these days, even the most conservative of the older men will admit that the girls pull their weight around the place. They're known to be "good with the stock" in just the same way that women have long been regarded as good horse handlers—probably because they are usually gentler. Most women in the outback will tell you that they have to be not only as good as the men, but better, if they want to earn their respect.

The outback has always been a tough place for women. In the late 1800s, George Essex Evans wrote the bush poem 'The Women of the West':

They left the vine-wreathed cottage and the mansion on the hill,
The houses in the busy streets where life is never still,
The pleasures of the city, and the friends they cherished best:
For love they faced the wilderness—the Women of the West.

Well have we held our father's creed. No call has passed us by.
We faced and fought the wilderness, we sent our sons to die.
And we have hearts to do and dare, and yet, o'er all the rest,
The hearts that made the Nation were the Women of the West.

These days, more women than ever are being lured inland to make the life-changing move to the outback. You'll find them all over the inland. They meet a good-looking fellow in Sydney or Brisbane, the Gold Coast or Cairns, and they don't look back. But whereas once the wife sat at home, or worse still in the stock camp, while the boys were mustering or droving, these days, she's more likely to be riding out there with them. There are stock camps in the north that are entirely run by women. Many of the contract musterers are female.

Contract mustering teams have become a mainstay of the modern pastoral industry. These days, most cattle stations depend on them to come in once or twice a year, reducing the number of permanent staff needed on a station and keeping the overheads down. The contract mustering team comes complete with horses, trucks and their own camp and canteen facilities. They're generally self-sufficient and often choose to live out in the paddocks, sleeping in their swags under the stars. They are the modern-day cowboys and cowgirls.

A couple of decades ago, a large cattle station would have had an on-station team of 20 to 30 station hands but these days the norm is usually fewer than five or six.

Cattle station stock camps are part of Australian folklore. They are used to reach the cattle in outlying areas—often 100 kilometres or more from the homestead. They can take the form of everything and anything, from the relative comfort of an unused manager's house or shed to nothing more than a waterhole and a few cattle yards in the middle of nowhere. Once, the station hands would move out to the stock camps and live there for days or weeks on end. Now, the station is more likely to use trucks to take the horses—already saddled and ready to go—out to the camps and come back each night so that the station hands can sleep in their own beds.

With dawn till dusk working days, most people turn in early. This means social life on the stations tends to be a few drinks in the evening with your workmates, supplemented with a trip to town every so often. When you live in the outback, going to town constitutes a big occasion. And town might be just a pub, a shop and a couple of houses reached along a corrugated track. Even visiting the neighbours can take half a day.

A life in the saddle has always been a rewarding job: full of adventure and a source of so much folklore, it's no wonder Australia's workers have been attracted to the lifestyle since the early days of settlement.

Whereas once the social life of the bush was rich with balls, picnics, inter-station cricket matches and tennis tournaments, these days social occasions have a narrower focus with horse sports being the driver.

Picnic races are still popular though. In countless rural towns and townships, the bush picnic races are a high spot on the social calendar. They bring together people scattered across vast distances who get few opportunities to socialise. It's a great time for dressing up. The picnic races are a long way from the 'Sport of Kings' held in the cities but the fashions of the field are just as hotly contested in the Kimberley as they are at Flemington.

By far the most popular get-together is the campdraft with the big events attracting competitors from all over the country. The cattle stations field teams because campdrafting fits in perfectly with station work.

This is a proudly Australian sport which is thought to have started in outback Queensland somewhere at the end of the 1800s as an informal competition between stockmen wanting to test their skills—or more specifically those of their horses. When drovers needed to select individual cattle from a mob to drive them to holding paddocks, the stockman would 'cut out' the beast from the mob. This was usually done when large mobs of cattle were mustered and held by a team of horsemen on the open plain, while the nominated rider did the 'cutting out'.

Eventually, it evolved into a fully fledged sport with rules and a course. The aim of the modern sport is to select a beast from a small mob of cattle and manoeuvre it to display the horse's ability to control the animal and block its attempts to follow its natural instincts in returning to the mob.

Points are scored by horse and rider for cut out, horse work and course completion, from a possible total of 100 points. A good campdrafter is not just a fine horseman or horsewoman, but has the skill to select from the mob a suitable beast that will run well.

The notion of an event that would test the full gamut of horse riding and management skills started with the Cloncurry Stockman's Challenge in the early 1980s. It is still regarded as one of the best judges of horse and rider and now there are challenges across Australia where stockmen and women compete in an array of challenges such as whip cracking, packhorse, bareback obstacle, cross country, shoeing and stock handling events. The key events include the Korroyong Man from Snowy River Challenge and the King of the Ranges Challenge in the Upper Hunter Valley.

Polocrosse, that peculiarly Australian version of an English sport, is also enjoying a resurgence. Dubbed 'king of the one-horse sport', it has a strong family following and matches take place most weekends. As the name implies, the game is a combination of polo and lacrosse. Polocrosse traces its origins back to the 1930s and the School of Equitation in the genteel Home Counties suburb of Kingston Vale, when it took place indoors with two players a side as an exercise for young riders to help develop their riding skills.

It was brought to Australia in 1938 by a Sydney couple, the Edward Hirsts, but it wasn't long before the Aussies made it their own, modified it and turned it into a more rambunctious outdoor sport filled with drama, spills and challenges—and very exciting to watch. Polocrosse is now being exported around the world. The biggest importer is, ironically, the place where the game began: England. Australia has successfully re-exported the sport back to the Home Counties.

Endurance riding is one of the world's fastest growing horse sports and Australia ranks among the top medal winning countries. Bush legend, the late R. M. Williams, together with his wife, Erica, is credited with sowing the seeds of the early sport. Through their magazine, *Hoofs and Horns*, they drew local attention to the first American Tevis Cup endurance ride and canvassed the notion of a similar event in Australia. Out of this was born the world endurance classic, the annual 160 kilometre Tom Quilty Gold Cup—named after the Kimberley cattleman who gave the money for a trophy.

The Quilty Cup objective is to test horse and rider: "100 miles (160 kilometres) on one horse in one day." Competitors start the ride at midnight and have 24 hours to cross the finishing line with their horse still fit and healthy. Held in winter in a different state each year, the Quilty is regarded as one of the world's toughest horse races with the very best international riders making an annual pilgrimage in search of a Quilty buckle. It

The Upper Hunter Valley's Muswellbrook Polocrosse Club has played host to numerous championships over the years, with this 'king of the one-horse sport' having a large family following (photo: Tim Clayton).

has been joined by other 'classics' including the 400 kilometre Shahzada marathon at St Albans north-west of Sydney and the Faraway Marathon at Imbil in Queensland's Sunshine Coast hinterland.

Endurance events of 80 kilometres are held on most weekends of the year across Australia and riders float their horses long distances in order to compete.

For many, it rekindles the spirit of the old bushmen. It gives present generations continuity with their past and exemplifies the 'never surrender' approach to adversity that Australians admire so much.

Imported from the USA—which borrowed it from Mexico—rodeo is now a popular Australian bush sport with a strong following. Travelling tent rodeos were a regular sight in the 1920s and 1930s, with circuit competitors and spectators alike having a go in the ring. Bushmen's carnivals originated in northern NSW in the 1920s and were well established by the 1930s. The end of World War II saw a revival of the carnivals and the birth of the tradition of donating proceeds to local charities. It was not until the 1940s and 1950s that rodeo came to be the spectacle it is today.

Getting medical assistance in the outback is a major issue that has been addressed in a uniquely Australian fashion. In remote homesteads, cattle stations, Aboriginal communities and the clusters of demountables that make up mining outposts, there is the medical chest—locked for security but ready for action. Not far away there is always a phone and on the wall next to it, a number. This is the hotline to the Royal Flying Doctor Service (RFDS)—the lifeline of the outback.

In an era when most doctors stopped making house calls years ago, the RFDS runs a 24-hour on-call service. It treated 73,000 patients by phone alone in 2005. If there is a child with a high temperature or someone has a sudden illness, there is a team of doctors and nurses rostered on and happy to help—they listen to problems, ask questions, give advice and prescribe the right medication. Each of the 90 items in the standard RFDS medical chest is numbered so there is no confusion when the doctor explains what is to be used and how. Regular audits ensure that everything is up to date and accounted for.

If it's an emergency—a stockman fallen off a horse, a car rolled on a dirt road, a baby arriving unexpectedly early—an aircraft carrying a medical team of pilot, flight nurse and medical officer will be dispatched and be alongside the patient, in most cases, within two hours.

On an average day across Australia, RFDS medical officers treat about 650 patients and transport more than 90 patients by air. The fleet of 50 aircraft covers more than 50,000 kilometres each day and nearly 20 million kilometres every year. This non-profit organisation is the oldest and largest airborne health service of its kind in the world.

The beginnings of the Royal Flying Doctor Service go back to 1917 when the Reverend John Flynn, who was Superintendent of the Australian Inland Mission, started to canvass ideas for a rapid medical evacuation service for the outback. Clifford Peel, a Victorian medical student, wrote to him outlining a plan using aerial ambulances. Tragically, Peel, a member of the Australian Flying Corps, was killed in France before his ideas were realised.

But the vision lived on. In 1928 the first Aerial Medical Service flight left Cloncurry for Mt Isa to pick up and return an injured youth. In 1942, the service was renamed the Flying Doctor Service and after a visit, the Queen approved the Royal prefix in 1955.

They're a feisty and resourceful lot, outback doctors. It comes with the territory. They are the closest thing you'll find to the traditional family GP who has all but disappeared from the city and suburbs but who most of us would love to still have. In the small townships dotted across the remoter regions of Australia, they are the linchpin of the communities they serve.

These doctors regularly make life or death decisions. Working without immediate support means they have to be surgeon, obstetrician, psychiatrist, dermatologist, cardiologist—you name it. In an age of specialisation, they are the supreme generalists. They are on call 24 hours a day and their patients love them for it.

If the doctors are revered, remote area nurses are the unsung heroes of the outback, often working in extreme conditions and in some of the loneliest places on earth. They provide almost all general healthcare in the most remote areas.

It is estimated there are about 5000 nurses working in the outback. The typical remote area nurse is older than those in the city and predominantly female. She has a long background in nursing and overwhelmingly she has a strong desire to make a difference to the world she lives in.

Remote area nurses could be living with an indigenous community in the Gibson Desert, on an island in the Torres Strait or in a tiny fishing township on the north coast of Western Australia. They deal with everything and anything that comes along. Often, they are working in dangerous situations: it is not unusual for an inexperienced and unsuspecting nurse to be caught up in domestic violence or family battles.

The Council of Remote Area Nurses of Australia (CRANA) offers support for people in the field. It provides training courses and offers professional advice as well as helping maintain an informal networking service for nurses so they can contact each other. More than anything, remote area nurses must be resourceful and capable and keen to use their own initiative. There is a high attrition rate. The job is very much a love it or hate it situation. Some people stay for decades, others are gone within the week.

Routinely, they deal with day-to-day illness problems and respond to emergencies, but much of their work is about introducing good lifestyle practices and nutrition to outlying indigenous communities. Prevention is the key, and their approach to health is based on the whole-of-life concept, encompassing physical, spiritual and emotional wellbeing of individuals, family, community and environment.

Like healthcare, education in the outback is dealt with resourcefully and efficiently. Especially in the early grades, it comes by way of the School of the Air. This icon of remote life has been operating for nearly half a century. It was the brainchild of Adelaide Miethke, vice-president of the South Australian wing of the Royal Flying Doctor Service and a former inspector of girls' schools, who recognised the possibilities of using the RFDS radio as a way of bringing the classroom into outback homes.

The first lessons were transmitted from the Alice Springs Flying Doctor Base in 1949 and the Alice Springs School of the Air was founded in 1951. Other schools followed. These days there are 12 School of the Air schools serving students dotted over 1.5 million square kilometres.

"The kids of the outback often learn to ride a horse as early as they learn to walk. Many can drive a car by the time they are 10. But give them a football and they're lost." The speaker is a remote station mum who is explaining why School of the Air holds regular get-togethers for students and their families and why the annual sports day is so important.

In each state, all students work from the same printed curriculum supplemented by a daily phone lesson with the teacher and the rest of the on-air class. Classes are kept small—usually less than 10—so that everyone can be included.

These days, the radio has given way to the computer. Many children learn on the internet. The federal government's Networking the Nation program, which began in 1996 and funded a multitude of state projects, has resulted in a huge uptake of the internet in the outback.

The Alice Springs School of the Air provides a good example of how technology is transforming education. Virtual lessons are conducted through the school's own internet service provider, using a satellite system. It also offers a 24-hour email service. Teachers and students can share information via video clips, music and PowerPoint presentations. Each student in grades 5 to 7 has a website, as does each teacher and each class. Before video, children new to the school didn't know what their classmates and teachers looked like. Now, they can put a face to the voice.

There is no other way to describe it: technology has revolutionised the bush. It could be argued that it is the greatest single benefit for the people of the outback since the Australian inland was opened up. Now, more than ever before, the remote lifestyle has moved closer to that of the city. These days, even in the most isolated spots, the party line and the local telephonist have been replaced with private phone lines and mobile phones—both generally available 24 hours a day. Newspapers are read on-line, and banking and other services are conducted via the computer—a far cry from dealing with a list of errands during infrequent trips to town.

Across the nation, you'll find everyone communicating with each other by email. Personal letters, business communications—they're all done on-line. Almost every aspect of daily life has been transformed through access to services such as e-banking and shopping. Information services, especially the weather report, are invaluable. Then there are all the leisure pursuits. The people of the bush can share the same on-line recreational activities as their city counterparts.

Technology is also playing a big part in making travel safer and quicker.

In the beginning, horses were the only way to get around. Camels were brought to Australia from Africa and India between 1840 and 1900 to move the heavy stuff across the inland deserts. But when man got the hang of the combustion engine and built railway lines across the inland the camels were turned loose to fend for themselves. Without predators and with ample grazing land, they survived and flourished. They went from being ships of the desert to being feral pests. With numbers estimated at about half a million there have been many calls to cull them. At last, though, it seems that camels are coming into their own again. Recent commercial camel sales in Queensland have seen a steady growth in interest and a shift in thinking. An estimated 10,000 camels are 'behind the wire' and in breeding programs with owners eyeing the Middle Eastern export markets.

These days, people travel the inland tracks in the latest four-wheel drives kitted out with high-tech equipment. Navigational electronics such as EPIRBS and GPS finders have made inland travel safer. There is also more traffic on the roads. Each year sees more tourists trundling up and down the highways and criss-crossing the continent on every outback track. Backpackers are exploring the wilder parts of Australia and grey nomads are discovering the continent they never knew before.

It is claimed that about 40 lives are lost each year on outback roads—mainly through mistakes like drinking, speeding, and swerving for wildlife. A handful of people go missing or get bogged and some lose their lives because they don't take enough water or don't stay with their vehicle. We have come a long way from the days of the early explorers, and the number of people who get lost and die are few and far between—but the outback remains a dangerous place.

The lifestyle of the outback is changing—and mostly for the better. While many of the old families have gone, new people have come in to take their place. Technology is transforming communications and transport. Getting across the empty spaces is quicker and safer. Burke and Wills would be shocked to see tourists lining up at the Dig tree—the very spot where they perished from lack of water a mere 150 years ago. In a relatively short space of time the outback has become somewhat friendlier and more accessible.

But much about inland Australia remains the same. The isolation is just as intense; the climate is as unpredictable and dangerous; the work is just as hard as ever and the days just as long. Despite the hardships of life and the remoteness there is an energy about the people that is both humbling and inspiring. The pioneering spirit is by no means gone. Unquestionably, their character is shaped by the land they inhabit.

And this is an ancient land. The ferociously empty plains and the red rock monoliths probably look much the same as they did 65 million years ago, bathed in the same strange luminous sheen of the huge outback moon. Some things will never change.

The full moon looms larger in the vast, empty outback. Here, it lights the way for a drover herding cattle near the central-western Queensland town of Barcaldine (photo: Sean Davey).

Cyclone Tracy, which hit Darwin on Christmas Eve, 1974, left 65 dead and a nation stunned by the images.

Weathering the extremes

Daniel Lewis

Australians don't need to have heard the haunting beauty of Dorothea Mackellar's poem 'My Country' to know that they live on a sunburnt continent of drought, flooding rains and many other spectacularly savage events.

Indeed, ours is an island that seems to specialise in extreme displays of nature which would not look out of place in the Old Testament—from hail storms to dust storms to raging floodwaters to locust plagues. Flooding alone serves up an average annual damage bill of $400 million a year, the Bureau of Meteorology says in its publication *Drought, Dust and Deluge: A Century of Climate Extremes in Australia*.

Probably the most famous flood in the recorded history of NSW hit the Hunter Valley in 1955, affording images so dramatic they were used in the movie *Newsfront*. In Maitland, more than 5000 homes were flooded and 15,000 people were evacuated. The disaster claimed 14 lives.

The Australian 24-hour rainfall record, established in 1893, is 907 millimetres, set at Crohamhurst north-west of Brisbane.

Cyclone Tracy—which left 65 dead and destroyed Darwin on Christmas Eve 1974—is Australia's most famous cyclone, but not the most deadly. When Mahina, a category 5 cyclone, hit north Queensland near Bathurst Bay on Cape York Peninsula on March 4, 1899 it killed more than 400 people and destroyed around 100 pearling boats.

Australia holds the world record—160 days—for the longest sequence of days with maximum temperatures equal to or above 100 degrees Fahrenheit (37.8 degrees Celsius). It was set in Western Australia's Marble Bar in 1923–24. The highest temperature recorded in Australia using standard observing techniques was 50.7 degrees Celsius at Oodnadatta in South Australia in 1960.

The Maitland floods. In 1955 **(top left and right)**, flooding in the town was so severe 14 lives were lost and survivors were forced to 'ride' their houses to safety; a resident clings to a street sign (photo: N. Alcova). During the recent floods of June, 2007 **(above left and right)**, the town was again submerged (photos: Peter Stoop and Andrew Sawatske).

Floods and bushfires provide cruelly stunning images, but heatwaves have accounted for more deaths in Australia than any other climatic event, the bureau notes. A 1939 scorcher killed 438 people in South Australia, Victoria and NSW.

At the other extreme, freezing conditions also take their toll. In 1900 snow fell across a vast area of NSW: trains were stranded and roofs in Bathurst collapsed under a metre of snow. The record for the lowest temperature recorded on the Australian mainland is minus 23 degrees Celsius at Charlotte Pass in the Snowy Mountains in 1994.

South-east Australia is one of the world's most fire-prone environments and its many disastrous bushfires have been well documented.

The 1982–83 drought and the subsequent Ash Wednesday bushfires claimed 75 lives and destroyed 2500 homes in Victoria and South Australia.

But because of Australia's size and sparse population, very few people would have heard of Australia's biggest fire. In 1974–75, 117 million hectares, spread across many areas of the inland—15 per cent of the country's land mass—burned after exceptional outback rainfall producing abundant grass and scrub was followed by a long dry spell.

In terms of the national economy, drought is the most costly climatic extreme. The modern nation was born in the midst of the 1895–1902 'Federation Drought'. That prolonged dry spell was so bad that the NSW government declared February 26, 1902, a day of "humility and prayer", such was the concern about Sydney's water supply.

The drought of 1944–45 was so intense it saw the Murray River stop flowing in places. But in terms of one-year rainfall deficiency the 1982–83 drought was the most severe of the 20th century, and the bureau says the drought from March 2002 to January 2003 was "comparable in severity and . . . extent with the droughts of 1902 and 1982–83"—except that the weather was even hotter.

With great droughts come great dust storms. In 1902, one was so bad that it delayed the mail coach from Hay to Deniliquin by nine hours. Another monster in 1944 resulted in Sydney having to turn on its street lights in the early afternoon and some country rail lines were buried up to a metre deep.

In 2006, record books had to be rewritten again. During the six months from June to November, the mighty Murray-Darling river system had inflows that were half those of the previous low in 1902 and only 7 per cent of the long-term average. There was an historic zero allocation of water for irrigators along the Murray, the dams of the Snowy scheme reached new lows and livestock that couldn't attract a bid at the saleyards were being shot.

Then compare 2006 to 1956. That year vast areas of the state were under water for months during the greatest flood modern Australia has known. The town of Wentworth, where the Murray and the Darling meet, erected a statue of a Massey Ferguson tractor to pay homage to the workhorse that helped build the levee banks that saved the community from being washed away.

Tiny Tilpa on the Darling had already been cut off by flood waters for five months when a *The Sydney Morning Herald* front page in August 1956 declared local postmaster, Fred Davidson, "the loneliest man in all the state".

The village's 15 other families had fled the inland sea long before and Davidson was there "living like Robinson Crusoe", with just wild pigs for company.

The Darling had already swollen to 80 kilometres wide, more flood water was coming and he did not expect anyone to return to the village until Christmas. "But there are plenty of Murray cod in the river. I can throw a line into it from my window," he told the *Herald*. "If you ever come up this way, drop in and I'll give you the best Murray cod you ever tasted."

There is no greater indicator of the extreme nature of Australia's climate than its biggest inland river system. The Murray-Darling catchment covers a million square kilometres and is Australia's breadbasket.

The writer Henry Lawson visited Bourke on the Darling in 1892–93 and witnessed the river's erratic moods, noting it was "either a muddy gutter or a second Mississippi". Sometimes the river stops flowing; at other times a Sydney Harbour's worth of water can flow past Bourke in a single day. The difference between its annual maximum and minimum flows is vastly greater than that of other major rivers like the Amazon, the Rhine or the Yangtze.

The Australian bush experiences weather extremes of near-Biblical proportions: a surreal street scene **(above left)** in the country town of Bathurst following a snow storm (photo: Brendan Esposito); the sun is almost obliterated by a dust storm as it blows through Mildura **(above right)**, on the border of New South Wales and Victoria (photo: Nick Moir).

In an effort to drought-proof the irrigation industry that provides so much of Australia's agricultural wealth, there are enough dams on the Murray-Darling system to store 1.5 times the annual average natural flows. We store more water per head of population than any other nation on earth, but it still hasn't been enough.

Australia might account for 5 per cent of the Earth's land mass, but it only gets 1 per cent of its rainfall and is the driest continent. Only 12 per cent of our rainfall becomes river flow.

Historian Michael McKernan says that "drought is the Australian story."

In his book, *Drought, The Red Marauder* published in 2005, McKernan cites Bureau of Statistics data which showed that the "most devastating" droughts occurred in 1895–1903, 1958–1968, 1982–83 and 1991–95.

McKernan reports that there were "major droughts" in 1864–66, 1880–86, 1888, 1911–16, 1918–20 and 1939–45. There were also "severe droughts" in 1922–23, 1926–29, 1933–38, 1946–49, 1951–52, 1970–72, 1976 and 1997–2000.

"Australia is, obviously, a dry continent," he says.

> *Drought is one of its biggest problems. But look at those years again—24 years in a century and a half of "devastating drought"; 22 years of "major droughts" and 23 years of "severe droughts". For nearly half the years since records began, across the country there has been some type of significant drought.*

McKernan argues that it was not until the 1980s that Australians finally came to terms with drought and seriously started preparing for it.

There was a severe, life-threatening drought in the first years of white settlement at Sydney Cove and McKernan says:

> *I am arguing that it has taken us 200 years to wake up to the simple fact that Australia is the driest continent. "Cultural baggage" is what historians call the ideas, prejudices and beliefs that migrants bring with them to a new land, a new life. In Australia the cultural baggage was so heavy, so great, that it took nearly 200 years to shift it.*

With global warming now an unarguable reality, how are we better preparing for and dealing with drought? The ways are many.

Some farmers are switching to more drought-tolerant breeds of African sheep. Others have given up on sheep altogether and switched to the even more drought-friendly wild goats that were already thriving on their arid land.

Farmers are storing more fodder, stocking their land more conservatively, using more scientific grazing rotations, taking far greater interest in weather records and long-range climate forecasts. They are replanting native vegetation such as old man saltbush which is drought hardy and on which stock can live in dry times.

As for cropping, scientists have already conventionally bred plants that are much more drought tolerant, with genetically modified research promising even more advances.

Ploughing is one of the mechanised world's oldest agricultural practices, but many farmers have now abandoned it.

By adopting no-tillage methods—where the ground is left undisturbed and the crop sown directly into the stubble of the previous season's harvest—farmers have been able to massively increase the amount of moisture that gets trapped in their soils.

Here is a fascinating irony: despite our dry land, Australia is one of the world's biggest net exporters of water. Each year we export products that consumed about 7.5 million megalitres of water. In order to achieve this, much of the Murray-Darling basin has seen its water resources over-allocated—that is, farmers have been given the right to remove more water than is environmentally sustainable.

Agriculture accounts for more than 70 per cent of Australia's water use and there are tens of thousands of kilometres of open channels wasting massive amounts of water through leakage and evaporation.

The Farmhand Foundation, in its *Talking Water* publication of 2004, says more efficient irrigation methods could save about 50 per cent of the water used on farms. Water is increasingly being piped to reduce losses and farmers are increasingly moving to much more efficient means of delivering water to their crops such as drip and centre pivot irrigation.

Some have shifted away from the most thirsty, flood-irrigated crops such as rice and cotton into products such as grapes and citrus that deliver more profit per megalitre.

Water trading is being encouraged so that Australia's most valuable resource finds its way to those who use it most efficiently.

Millions of dollars are being spent looking at the impacts of climate change on agriculture and how farmers can adapt. There is a strong school of thought that Australia's innovative farm sector will come to terms with what is likely to be a hotter and drier climate, but others warn severe change could come too quickly for many to adapt.

When times turn dry, many farmers still resort to old-fashioned safety nets like the Long Paddock: roadside stock routes available to all.

The iconic stock routes provide a fodder reserve that can keep animals alive until the rains finally fall at home. Droving is an ancient practice and McKernan took the name of his book from some Henry Lawson lines:

Our Andy's gone to battle now
'Gainst drought the red marauder;
Our Andy's gone with cattle now
Across the Queensland border.

In his 1889 poem 'Clancy of the Overflow', Banjo Paterson painted a romantic picture of droving:

As the stock are slowly stringing,
Clancy rides behind them singing,
For the drover's life has pleasures
that the townsfolk never know.

But in 'Saltbush Bill', Paterson captured the other side of droving on western stock routes: he describes a job that required rat cunning and a fierce right hook to keep the mob alive during a Big Dry. There was no "vision splendid of the sunlit plains extended" for Saltbush Bill; just a constant battle with the squatters and the laws of the Long Paddock.

Now this is the law of the Overland that all in the west obey,
A man must cover with travelling sheep a six-mile stage a day;
But this is the law which the drovers make, right easily understood,
They travel their stage where the grass is bad, but they camp where the grass is good;
They camp and they ravage the squatter's grass till never a blade remains,
Then they drift away as the white clouds drift on the edge of the saltbush plains.

In recent years, out on the NSW stock routes, desperation has bred desperate measures. Drovers have taken to each other with stock whips to win the best bit of feed, rocks have been thrown at cars that failed to slow down for stock and the rangers that police the Long Paddock have had to take conflict resolution training.

Indeed, the Big Dry has seen things get so edgy between drovers, farmers, motorists and rural lands protection board rangers that a new Drovers' Code of Conduct has even been published.

Clancy would be shocked. But Saltbush Bill would probably just grin and pretend he couldn't read.

A farmer pushes through a dust storm on the road between Hungerford and Bourke (photo: Rick Stevens).

Climate: the future

Pamela Robson

Australia's farmers and pastoralists don't need reminding that they are at the mercy of the weather. They're accustomed to battling nature at her most violent. Since settlement, they've faced the rigours and hardships of drought and flood, dust storms and tropical cyclones. But now they have something else to contend with: climate change.

This is an issue that is of such monumental—some say biblical—proportions and which carries such profound consequences for humankind that it has taken years for the global community to even begin to come to terms with it. Governments, business and some sections of the scientific community have been less than willing to accept the prospect of a warming planet. Its causes, the effects it will have on our future and the potentially catastrophic weather crises that threaten our lives, have led to much emotional debate. The various climate models, the statistics and their implications are complex and easily manipulated. And it is no surprise that some sections of business have been trenchantly and vocally opposed. But now we have a former US vice president, the British Treasurer, the Pentagon and even the CEO of the world's largest oil company urging action.

Historically, 2007 will go down as the year the world woke up to climate change.

Those who live close to the land are least likely to be surprised at the scientific confirmation. For many years now, Australians who live in the bush have observed that the weather is changing. Certainly, they have been forced to live with the already evident consequences in a much more direct fashion than those of us who live in the cities.

Over the millennia, the world has experienced huge variances in climate—from tropical periods to ice ages and everything in between. What is new is the speed at which we are heating up the planet. Increasingly, the evidence points to man's activities. Some of the changes in climate cannot be explained in any other way. Early in 2007, the United Nations Intergovernmental Panel on Climate Change (IPCC) stated that it was 90 per cent likely that climate change was man-made. Certainly, the evidence is there for increased atmospheric carbon dioxide levels: they are 35 per cent higher than in pre-industrial times.

In the past 100 years, the global temperature has increased by about 0.65 degrees Celsius with nine of the 10 warmest years recorded during the most recent decade. There has also been a warming of the lower atmosphere and the upper ocean. Temperatures at the poles have risen. The arctic ice sheet has been reduced in area by about 15 per cent and in thickness by almost 50 per cent. Sea levels have risen by about 20 millimetres each decade over the last50 years.

The global warming process is much more complex than simply 'warming things up'. In fact, some places are expected to become cooler. As the planet heats up so do the oceans, and as water heats it expands. As a consequence, sea levels rise. Melting ice at the poles adds to the increase. Ocean currents are affected and that is when major weather patterns like El Niño come into the equation.

The UN's IPCC predicts the planet will be warmer by up to 4 degrees Celsius within 100 years. And it is generally agreed that at least a 1 degree Celsius rise is inevitable. Sea levels are forecast to rise by between 0.18 metres and 0.59 metres over the same period.

Predictions for Australia include a warming of between 0.4 degrees Celsius and 2 degrees Celsius between 1990 and 2030 and an increase of between 1 degree Celsius and 6 degrees Celsius by 2070.

In day-to-day terms, this means more hot days over 35 degrees Celsius—up to three times as many by 2070. Higher temperatures will lead to increased water evaporation.

According to current predictions, much of the southern part of Australia will become drier while the north will be subject to more rain and, ultimately, flooding. There will also be an increase in the frequency and duration of extreme climatic events such as cyclones, rain storms, floods and droughts. The CSIRO is researching the likely impact of global warming on the frequency and severity of El Niño, as well as on tropical cyclone behaviour.

Their scientists have predicted a decrease in the amount of winter rainfall in Australia's south by as much as 8 per cent by 2030. At the same time the weather systems that produce heavy rainfall in northern and central Australia are likely to become more intense. In north-western Australia, annual heavy rainfall intensity has increased by more than 50 per cent since 1910. Global warming also spells substantial flooding around the Australian coastline from rising sea levels combined with big tides. This not only threatens the human population living on the edge of the continent, but also the wildlife ecosystems that depend on freshwater habitats near the coast.

So what does all this mean for Australia's farming sector and ultimately, the consumer—in other words, all of us?

Overarchingly, the south will struggle with drier winters and springs while the northern savannah country will enjoy consistently better seasons. However, the north will have to contend with more cyclones and floods.

Climate experts believe that areas south of a line drawn between Sydney and Perth will become hotter and drier. This means that entire farming regions of NSW and Victoria could be rendered vulnerable—if not unviable. Areas like the east-central Murray-Darling Basin—already struggling under drought—could face even greater water shortages. And most of Australia's irrigation farmers are in the Murray-Darling. As the climate changes, the southern part of the basin is forecast to experience significantly reduced water levels, and this will directly and adversely affect a large number of irrigation practices.

Hardly a section of rural industry would be left untouched by water shortages created by climate change, from the wheat belt of NSW to the Victorian dairy industry and the wine industry. Cotton operations in particular require a substantial water supply and a shortage would damage the industry.

Warmer temperatures are also expected to affect Australia's fruit growers. A rise of only a degree or so could reduce yields and the quality of some fruit varieties that need periods of cold weather to grow, such as stone fruit and apples.

And if that's not enough, insects, pests and weeds are predicted to spread in the warmer conditions.

Less rainfall in winter and spring will impact on pasture growth in the southern areas making cattle properties in NSW and Victoria less viable. By contrast, rainfall in the northern regions will benefit pastoralists. Given that higher carbon dioxide levels will promote plant growth, beef production in the north could be expected to increase.

This means the beef cattle industry could move north with stations in northern Queensland and the Northern Territory becoming prime properties while their southern counterparts struggle. All this will have an effect on production, the numbers of cattle, cattle breeds and where cattle are sourced.

Already the southern sheep industry, devastated by drought, expects a cutback of about 5.5 million during 2007 to leave a national flock of about 95 million. The southern cattle industry is expected to see a 2.4 per cent cutback in 2007—or about a 700,000 fall in the herd numbers.

Ultimately, the impact of climate change on farm production will have huge ramifications for the household shopping bill and the availability and range of food products.

Australia was dubbed "the lucky country" in 1964 by Donald Horne. He penned these words with some irony and the phrase sits well with us today. For many years, we have grown accustomed to enjoying a wide range of top quality fresh produce at low prices. In world terms, Australians are very spoilt. The abundance of cheap fresh food means we also have some of the best and cheapest restaurants and food outlets on the planet.

But already Australians are experiencing food price increases as the result of cyclones and drought. Is this a foretaste of things to come?

Cyclone Larry's destruction of the north Queensland banana crop in early 2006 led to price hikes of more than 250 per cent. And while carrot growers faced high water charges during the patchy drought in south-east Queensland, cheaper carrots were being trucked into Brisbane supermarkets from Tasmania.

This farmer—photographed at the Bendigo Livestock Exchange with his dogs—contemplates selling his sheep and cattle as tough conditions continued due to a drought that swept Victoria (photo: Simon O'Dwyer).

Drought in the southern farming areas also helped to push up the nation's food bill. In mid to late 2006, Australia saw the largest quarterly increase in food prices in 23 years. The Murray-Darling—often called Australia's food bowl—had set records with the driest five-year sequence on record.

In the middle of 2006, the Australian Bureau of Statistics announced that the food price index rose 4.1 per cent in June over the previous quarter, and had risen more than 8.3 per cent on the previous year—the highest increase in food prices in consecutive quarters in 23 years and the largest year-on-year jump in 17 years. During the period, fruit prices rose by 52 per cent.

In the latter part of 2006, food prices soared 10 per cent. Lamb and beef prices rose by 30 per cent in some parts of Australia. The price of a loaf of bread rose by 10 per cent due to a 40 per cent surge in flour prices. Vegetable prices increased by 30 per cent. Orange prices rose from $80 to $200 a tonne, with inevitable price hikes on orange juice.

Of all the challenges posed by climate change, the single most important issue facing farmers is water shortage. The drought in the south and the dwindling of the beleaguered Murray-Darling have already led to a battle between the southern states and Queensland over water. The debate centres on the vast Cubbie station in Queensland's Condamine-Balonne region which is the largest cotton growing operation in the southern hemisphere. Its dams can store as much water as Sydney Harbour.

The corporate owners of Cubbie claim theirs is an environmentally sustainable operation. That doesn't cut it with the NSW growers and graziers who rely on the floods of the Condamine-Balonne system to sustain their pastures. They say it's a case of one state allowing a development with total disregard for downstream users in another state.

The environmentalists also have a view. They believe that water shortages are less about drought and more about long-term conditions caused by far too much water being given to agriculture instead of the environment.

At the start of 2007, Prime Minister John Howard announced a $10 billion plan to save the Murray-Darling Basin and to take the responsibility of water out of the hands of the states. This did not please the states, especially South Australia, but it did satisfy some environmentalists who said the state governments had acted in the interests of their own farmers rather than the national interest.

In many areas the rural sector is also battling governments who need water for expanding urban areas. The drought in parts of the fast-growing population belt of south-east Queensland couldn't have come at a worse time for local farmers—just when they were negotiating water allocations with the Department of Natural Resources and Mines as part of the Council of Australian Governments' National Water Initiative.

On the face of it, the initiative is a sensible one. It was started in the mid 1990s to provide farmers with security over the water they are able to use. It replaced the old-style, fixed-term water licences which had no guarantee of renewal, with perpetual, secure and tradable water access entitlements—rather like freehold property title—for a share of the available water in their area.

Some farmers in the south-east Queensland region have ended up being offered much less water than they had historically been using. They are aggrieved because they believe they are being asked to risk the viability of their farming operations in favour of urban expansion. Clearly, balancing the needs of all sectors is set to become an increasingly difficult dilemma.

Much of the debate around climate change has centred on the short-term costs of intervention versus the long-term cost of not taking action. Around the world, countries are being urged to take immediate action. Given that greenhouse gas-producing fossil fuels such as coal and oil underpin our economy, Australia has much at stake.

Australia's mining industry is under fire from all sides. The possibility of carbon taxes on the mining industry is under discussion by state governments. In the Upper

The future of farming depends on sustainable energy, whether from controversial wind farms **(above left)** such as the massive one near Ararat (photo: Joe Armao), or from solar dishes like the ones installed at the Aboriginal community of Hermannsburg **(above right)**, south-west of Alice Springs (photo: Glenn Campbell).

Hunter Valley one of NSW's largest coalmining companies, Centennial Coal, has been battling local residents near Muswellbrook over a proposal to build the second largest open cut coalmine in the state. The battle is intense not only because of land use issues but because of the draining and damage to underground aquifers and other areas of the water supply.

When it comes to alternative energy sources, Australia is regarded as being better placed than most because of the combination of sunshine and gas in central Australia and a relatively short transmission distance to South Australia which is connected to the Australian energy grid.

Australia contributes only about one per cent of global greenhouse gas emissions. However, scientists and others warn that does not mean we shouldn't act speedily and effectively. They point out that many European countries are in a similar situation and the world needs to act collectively. The United States in particular is being asked to show leadership as the world's superpower. The USA contributes about a quarter of the world's greenhouse gases, although the share from China, India and other developing countries is also growing. Within the next decade, China is expected to surpass the United States as the world's largest emitter of greenhouse gases. India, another country of one billion-plus people, faces the same challenge of how to develop economically without ruining its environment.

Unquestionably, climate change has wide ranging and prolonged ramifications for Australia's rural sector. But our rural community has a long history of resilience, adaptability and strength of character. As one cattle farmer commented: "It's not about losing life as we know it, rather about how we can start changing and adapting for everyone's benefit."

It won't be the first time the bush has taken a collective breath and 'given it a go.'

The woolshed takes pride of place on the farm, with shearers filling its noisy interior for a few weeks a year.

Dynasties past and present

Nigel Austin

"Cattle kings you call us. Then we are kings in grass castles that may be blown away upon a puff of wind."

When outback pioneer Patrick (Patsy) Durack uttered his immortal words to a newspaper correspondent in the 1870s, he could scarcely have imagined that they would still ring true across Australia's farming landscape more than 130 years later. A lot has changed to make Australian agriculture a more sustainable industry than in Durack's day in the Kimberley region of north Western Australia. But even the most unexpected events—such as the drying up of the Murray River system in 2006–07—can still occur to thwart the most carefully laid plans.

Nevertheless, agriculture is a vastly different industry in the 21st century than it was in Durack's day with the arrival of the age of professional farming. Not only has Australia moved from an agricultural-based economy to a modern industrial nation; the way of farming has changed dramatically. Today, the industry is far more integrated into the modern $120 billion food industry, while it is also significantly more diversified than it was even 30 years ago. The profitability of large, professional agricultural operations is as good as any form of investment and even better in a number of cases.

Agriculture has been the cornerstone of the Australian nation since the First Fleet landed at Sydney Cove in 1788. Its success is a remarkable feat with the nation becoming one of the world's leading agricultural producers in little more than 200 years. Australia grows some of the cleanest and greenest food available, while our producers are among the most efficient, innovative and technologically advanced in the world. What we grow has changed dramatically in the past 50 years because of the transformation in what we eat. But Australia's place in the world remains, perhaps more than any other country, as an exporter, both of raw commodities and, increasingly, higher-value foods.

Since the mid 1800s, mining has at times vied with agriculture as the nation's main source of economic stability. The first metal mine in Australia was started in South Australia in 1839 in the Glen Osmond hills, a modern-day suburb of Adelaide. Copper mines followed at Kapunda in 1844 and in surrounding regions with the rich lode becoming that colony's number one export by 1850. Soon gold was discovered at Bathurst in NSW, creating Australia's first great gold rush. It was quickly followed by similar finds in the Ballarat region of Victoria, and for a time in the 1850s, mining became Australia's most important industry.

But as the gold fields ran out, the mineral wealth declined and Australia returned to ride on the sheep's back for the next 100 years. It was a ride that carried Australia grandly, although by the 21st century it had run its course, with the sheep flock reaching a 60-year low in 2007. By then mining had returned in a big way, to soar past agriculture in value as the wealth beneath Australia's topsoil was finally uncovered. Farm exports earned 90.2 per cent of Australia's merchandise exports in 1950–51 and mining did not equal the wealth created by the rural sector until 1977–78. But by 2005–06 it was worth $109.5 billion (59 per cent of merchandise exports) compared with rural exports worth $28.5 billion (20 per cent of the total).

While the rural landscape has changed greatly since the squattocracy era and the days of fabulous wealth in the 19th century, the new rural land barons rely as much on professionalism as their forebears did on cheap land and labour. At the forefront of modern agriculture are the producers such as Ingham's Chickens who run integrated businesses from farm to consumer, while there are numerous large producers in feedlotting, grain, cotton, grape growing, forestry, horticulture and aquaculture. Many of these operators and indeed a number of the important industries of today did not exist in any substantial form in Australia prior to the 1960s.

The largest rural operations are to be found in the nation's biggest individual rural

Australia's original 'cattle king' **(above left)**, Sir Sidney Kidman (1857–1935); the Kidman Corporation controls the largest land area in Australia. The Marshall brothers **(above right)**, in 1930, with a large nugget of gold.

industry, beef cattle, worth $7.2 billion in 2005–06. Arguably the success story of Australian agriculture in the past two decades, the major producers have enjoyed fabulous wealth gains through rising land values in recent years, based partly on higher beef prices due to the marketing success of Meat and Livestock Australia. The large northern pastoral business, in particular, appears set for further success due to its base in the more reliable higher rainfall tropical zone. While the "kings in grass castles" epithet used by Patsy Durack to describe the early beef barons seemingly remains as true today as it was all those years ago, the industry is in fact more reliable and profitable than ever before. Numerous northern pastoralists, including the shrewd, the large and the committed, are making considerable money from cattle.

In the early days the major producers included people such as W. J. T. 'Big' Clarke, James 'Hungry' Tyson, and then Sir Sidney Kidman: men who became so wealthy they owned large swathes of land and held vast fortunes. Today, the big are still big, but include a mix of old rural families and city businessmen. And they are more likely to be found in northern Australia than in the south.

The ranks of the nation's largest cattle producers have involved a continually changing group of names. In the past few decades one-time giants of the industry such as CSR, the Hooker Corporation (which once owned the mighty Victoria River Downs station), the Vestey, Angliss and Coutts families, King Ranch, Tancred Brothers, Brian Oxenford, N. M. Rural Enterprises and the Colonial Agricultural Company, have all left the industry. Likewise, legendary pioneering families including the Duracks, Quiltys and Emanuels have left the northern beef industry. In more recent years, death by accident, changing corporate priorities and a whole host of reasons have combined to bring rapid change to the list of largest producers.

The one constant has been S. Kidman and Co, owned by the descendants of the legendary cattle king, Sir Sidney Kidman. The Kidman operation still controls the largest land area in Australia with 11.92 million hectares and 200,000 cattle in a good year. Included among its 19 holdings is Anna Creek station on the south-western corner of Lake Eyre in South Australia. This 23,888 square kilometre cattle station runs 16,000 cattle in good times under the watchful eye of manager Randall Crozier.

The young Sid Kidman bought his first station, Owen Springs, in the Northern Territory at the age of 23 after running away from home in Adelaide at the age of 15. By the time of his death in 1935, Sir Sidney held a financial interest in 3.5 per cent of the Australian continent, an area larger than Victoria, and was running between 500,000 and 650,000 cattle. Kidman and Co, under the chairmanship of John Ayers, a great grandson of Sir Sidney Kidman, and chief executive Greg Campbell, remains at the forefront of the industry through shrewd management and clever strategies.

For about three decades from the 1960s, the Stanbroke Pastoral Company ruled the roost as Australia's largest cattle company, building an ever growing herd from scratch under the astute guidance of a series of businessmen such as Sir James Balderstone, at different times its managing director and chairman. But then the AMP's changing corporate requirements saw it sell off the empire for $417.5 million plus debt in 2003 to a conglomerate comprising Victorian Peter Menegazzo, a group of Queensland cattle producers headed by grazier Peter Hughes, and Hungry Jack's founder Jack Cowan. That ownership ended in 2004 with Menegazzo buying out his partners before tragically dying in a light plane crash in late 2005. The resulting operation, today run by his surviving family, is a smaller business at 200,000 cattle on 12 stations.

The new king of the beef cattle industry is the Elders Australia Ltd-backed Australian Agricultural Company with about 550,000 cattle on 25 vast northern stations covering 8.6 million hectares. Listed on the Australian Stock Exchange in 2001 with the aim of producing prime beef on its northern stations and gaining the highest value for its end product, it has been a success through rapid expansion and shrewd marketing. Its fascinating life started in the 1820s under an Act of England's Parliament and by Royal Charter when it was granted 1 million acres (404,685 hectares) of land for the cultivation and improvement of waste lands in the colony of New South Wales.

The nation's major cattle operators include some of Australia's biggest business names such as the Packer and Holmes à Court families. The Packers' Consolidated Pastoral Company runs 260,000 cattle on 17 stations, mainly in northern Australia, while managing other stations. The Holmes à Courts' Heytesbury Beef runs 150,000 cattle on eight stations, while other major players include the recently established Georgina Pastoral Holdings and Investments headed by Peter Hughes with 200,000 cattle on 14 stations. The top grouping includes the North Australia Pastoral Company with about 185,000 head followed by Great Southern Beef with 180,000 cattle, Don McDonald's MDH Pty Ltd with 160,000 cattle, and the Acton family's The Acton Land and Cattle Co with 150,000 cattle.

These 10 companies run more than 2.2 million cattle on 53 million hectares, a land area larger than Germany and almost as big as France. Collectively, their holdings amount to 10 per cent of all agricultural land in Australia. The value of their operations has increased immeasurably in the past decade due to land prices rising by up to 100 per cent—more in some cases—along with far greater stability in the modern beef industry.

The long fight for Aboriginal land rights took its toll on activist Eddie Mabo **(above left)**; he died in 1992, just months before the successful court ruling. Gladys Tybingoompa **(above right)**, of the Wik people, does a victory dance outside the High Court in Canberra after the 1996 Wik Decision (photo: Andrew Campbell).

A crucial role in the northern cattle industry's development in the early days was the work carried out by Aboriginal stockmen, without whom many pastoralists would have struggled to handle the heavy workload. Among the families who enjoyed a close relationship with the Aborigines on their stations, providing food and shelter for many years, was the Durack family. Their long and abiding friendship with the local Aboriginal group was portrayed in Dame Mary Durack's book *Kings in Grass Castles*.

But undermining the relationship between landowners and Aborigines was the absence of a treaty or any type of property law for Britain's settlement of Australia. The right of Aboriginal people to land has since been formally recognised in numerous legal and political ways, following long and hard fought battles. This eventuated in the 1982 Australian High Court Mabo decision which gave Common law recognition to Aboriginal people and their right to possess and enjoy their traditional lands. This decision found that Native Title existed where people could prove a continuing traditional connection to the land and where governments had not extinguished that connection.

By 2007, more than 15 per cent of the Australian continent has been granted to Aborigines and Torres Strait Islanders, either through Native Title claims or commercial acquisitions. This includes nearly half of the Northern Territory since the introduction of the 1976 Aboriginal Land Rights (Northern Territory) Act. Aboriginal-owned land in South Australia includes more than 80 rural properties covering 20 per cent of the state. In Western Australia, Aboriginal-owned land has reached 14 per cent, while the amount is a few per cent of Queensland and negligible in NSW, Victoria and Tasmania.

The most famous Aboriginal-owned property is Elsey station, near Mataranka in the Northern Territory, made famous by Jeannie Gunn in her outback classic *We of the Never Never*. Elsey was formally handed over to the Mangarrayi Aboriginal people, who have lived in the region for thousands of years, in February 2000. The handover coincided with a new-found pride and spirit among the Mangarrayi people who live next door to the station at the Jilkminggan Aboriginal Community. Six Aboriginal stockmen work on the property, of which the Mangarrayi people are extremely proud because it has given them a voice and an identity.

Despite the recent downturn in the wool industry, it was the backbone of the nation's economy for its first 170 years—and is still the only option for many dry-land farmers. Here, workers unload wool bales in 1930.

The 520,000 hectare Elsey was purchased by the Northern Land Council for $4.2 million in 1991 and converted to inalienable freehold title in 2000. The beautiful station is one of the most picturesque and best-watered properties in northern Australia. The Roper River runs through it for about 100 kilometres and spreads into large wetlands that have never been dry. The money made by Elsey goes back into running the station, while ownership of Elsey is also helping to provide employment and training for Aboriginal people in important station skills.

The backbone of the national economy for much of the nation's first 170 years, the wool industry, has declined considerably since the Reserve Price Scheme for wool was abandoned in 1990. The wool industry accounted for 80 per cent of Australia's exports as recently as the 1950s and earned export income of more than $6 billion in 1989. By contrast, wool exports in 2007 are worth$2.5 billion with the national wool clip down to its lowest level since the 1940s.

The impact has seen considerable wealth dissipate throughout regional Australia, and from many rural families. Nothing devastated rural Australia more than the decline of wool in the 1990s with small inland towns around the nation dwindling as the impact struck them. Populations dropped as people moved to the major cities and coastal areas with banks, government departments and other businesses deserting small country towns.

Nevertheless, wool remains important in many dry land farming regions around Australia where it is often the only option, and it remains viable for large efficient producers. Recovery from drought, strong demand from China and the increasing focus on meat, all promise a better future for the wool sector and the major wool producers. They include a range of dedicated rural families and modern agricultural companies operating large pastoral runs.

At the forefront are Clyde Agriculture, the Kahlbetzer family's Twynham Agricultural Group, the MacLachlans' Jumbuck Pastoral, A. J. and P. A. McBride, Tom Brinkworth and the Mutooroo Pastoral Company. Possibly the largest sheep flock is run by Clyde Agriculture, owned by the United Kingdom's Swire Group, with a flock of several hundred thousand sheep on properties in Queensland and NSW. Its sheep operation includes Thylungra station in western Queensland, settled by Patrick Durack and the starting point for the mobs of cattle driven by his sons and cousins to start their extensive holdings in the east Kimberley in the 1880s.

Other major wool operations include the McBride family's A. J. and P. A. McBride, a specialised operation with sheep stations through South Australia's pastoral zone and at Esperance, Western Australia. Wool remains a major business in much of South Australia's vast pastoral belt where cattle are unsuited, with pastoralists including the McBrides, MacLachlans, Morgans and others running large efficient operations.

Despite the decline of wool, the diversification of the agricultural sector has seen a number of new grain types provide new wealth in cropping regions. Additionally, cotton has become a major new crop for Australia since the 1960s, while wine production has expanded dramatically since 1990 with the value of exports growing from about $100 million to $3 billion in 2007.

Major producers abound in modern Australian agriculture where scale is as important as any factor in modern success. In dairy farming, Dairy Holdings Ltd has turned the historic Woolnorth property on the north-west tip of Tasmania into a major dairy operation, milking more than 15,000 cows on 23 farms. And Tasmania is the location of the Pye family's 3000 cow dairy operation at Rushy Lagoon on the north-eastern tip of the island. The Pye family also runs one of the nation's largest potato growing businesses at Parilla in the Murraylands region of South Australia where it was among the pioneers of a new irrigation industry in the early 1990s. Its own potato crop yields about 50,000 tonnes a year. At the same time the region has become a major new irrigation province, growing crops as valuable as the Ord River Scheme in north-west Western Australia, but it remains little known to the public.

In cotton, the Cubbie Group has emerged as the nation's largest grower with the potential to produce nearly 300,000 bales in Queensland in a good year. Some of the nation's largest farming operations have emerged in grain growing with the Harris family from Rowena in NSW cropping 50,000 hectares of wheat as well as other crops. Large farming operations also exist in grape growing, forestry, horticulture and increasingly aquaculture where tuna farming at Port Lincoln in South Australia is leading the way with a value of $200 million to $300 million a year.

In contrast to the major agricultural operations, many small family farmers are finding it increasingly difficult to continue on small holdings, without seeking income from off-farm work or investments. Leading business forecaster Phil Ruthven from IBIS World says the lack of money in running small farm operations has made young people increasingly reluctant to take over their parents' farms. "Farming has reached the end of the road where the young generation is no longer prepared to farm for little return," Mr Ruthven says. "Farming was a business until the 1950s, but then it became a way of life."

An increasing number of young people who return to farming often do so armed with university degrees or qualifications from agricultural colleges to better equip them for the challenging environment ahead. Hawkesbury, Orange, Gatton, Marcus Oldham, Glenormiston, Dookie, Tocal, Longerenong and Roseworthy agricultural colleges are some of the institutions which have trained many of Australia's modern-day farmers.

Small family farms are no longer attractive for many with steadily rising costs, often static returns, low salaries and hard work. Ruthven argues that a farmer would need to have assets of $3.5 million to earn $102,000, the average income of a city couple. But the average income of farming families in 2005–06 was only $45,000 a year: half the average city income in Australia.

Newcomers are increasingly embarking on careers in agriculture in different ways which enable them to make a return of 15 per cent on capital rather than 3 per cent.

Strategies involved include not owning land or machinery. Ruthven says:

> *What I have found among the young ones is a number inherited farms, but they have then gone out and leased a lot more land to make it more viable. They are also contracting a lot more of their work rather than sinking $300,000 into harvesting equipment that is hardly ever used. The hope with the young is that we are seeing an end of an era with the family farm as we know it because they are finding new ways of doing it.*

With about 120,000 farmers in Australia, Ruthven suggests the number may not slip much further: "What we are starting to see is a lot of new agricultural industries emerging such as aquaculture and hydroponics," he says. "We may see 30,000 wool and wheat farmers disappear, but the number will be made up by high intensity agriculture."

Companies such as Timbercorp Limited and Heytesbury Beef are good examples of agricultural companies of the future where the improved structure and scale of operations will ensure new generation farm workers are paid better than in the past. The return to full employment in Australia is expected to hasten the change in agriculture towards improved business structures. This trend is leading to a rapidly decreasing number of farms with a turnover of less than $100,000, while the number earning more is increasing steadily. The Farm Policy Research Institute highlighted the contribution of agriculture to the national economy. While it only contributes 3.2 per cent of Gross Domestic Product in a good year, when food and fibre value-adding sectors are included, more than 12 per cent of the economy relies on agriculture.

At the same time the rural sector is providing returns as good as any business sector with much of the return coming from capital appreciation. The farm sector is facing the conundrum that property values appear to be inflated for the average farmer, but for the top operators, values are such that they still provide a good return.

Many of the smaller farms on the edges of the big cities and towns are generally vastly different to the professional farms, in both returns and operation. More and more small farmers around Australia are sharefarming, or running their farms on the weekend while they seek work off-farm. Increasingly, they are finding work in the nation's mining sector, particularly in Western Australia, Queensland and South Australia, where the world's biggest uranium mine, BHP's Olympic Dam, is often said to be run by farmers. With an estimated 30,000 farmers leaving the industry in the past 15 years, for those who remain, close to half earn about one-third of their income off-farm.

The new and exciting era for farming includes farming operations that are far smarter and more technologically clever and even more integrated with their markets than ever before. A constant search for new ways of running farms to improve productivity is the only way to combat the constant decline in commodity prices that has lasted for at least the past 100 years. The new ways of the past decade that have made farming far different to the old horse and cart days include minimum and no-till cropping and a rapid uptake in Global Positioning Satellite navigation technology in tractors to make cropping work far more precise. And before too long, the driverless tractor is expected to be a fact of life as new age farmers increasingly run their farms from the office.

Rising corporate investment is also occurring rapidly in recognition of the high returns that are possible from large professionally run farms, while new financing methods are being used for a growing number of modern operations. The farms of the future will also include more fish farms as the world's supply from the wild rapidly diminishes. And they will include a rapidly escalating number of intensive livestock operations producing pork, chicken and beef and more intensive hydroponic greenhouse farms utilising new, environmentally smart technology.

The future is also likely to entail success on the last great frontier, the far north, where many have tried in the past with bucket-loads of money, but few have succeeded. Yet as southern water shortages increase, the drift north is inescapable. Consider this: while the Murray-Darling Basin receives about 23,000 gigalitres of run-off a year, the three major river systems of northern Australia carry 280,000 gigalitres. Optimism about the future of the north is consolidating amid increasing fears of food shortages in some parts of the world, particularly countries such as Japan and China.

Australia's agricultural innovators recognise that change is inescapable. For the brave, the rewards promise to be as lucrative as they have ever been, if not more so.

Children dance in the dust swirled up by a tractor on their farm near Birchip, Victoria (photo: Simon O'Dwyer).

Rebirth of the bush

Pamela Robson

They are into cheese, pigs, herbs, goats, orchards, fish, organics—even chutney and spices—anything they can produce from a few hectares. They are starting up new businesses in country towns, they are buying into existing ones, or they are taking their city businesses with them and working via the internet. They are called treechangers. It's been a long time coming but after decades of seachanging it seems we're finally turning our backs on the city and the beach and looking towards the country for our future. There's a buzz in the air as country towns and regions across Australia come back to life.

Because the bush is not just about farming and the outback; it is also about the thousands of country towns and villages scattered across the broad coastal strip around much of the continent.

Treechangers are on course to reform the connections between the country and the city. These days, the talk is all about diversity between rural regions replacing the city–country divide.

As is the way with large-scale social change, this revival of enthusiasm for the bush is the result of innumerable interweaving factors that have gathered momentum around the world. The search for a sense of community and a retreat from the urban pace of the 21st century are the main drivers. This is not new. Throughout history, people have sought refuge in the simple life, either as groups or as individuals. What's different about this social phenomenon is that we have the technology to make life in the country as comfortable as life in the city.

Typically, it is the artists and free thinkers who lead social revolution and the rest of us follow. Certainly, over the past decade, we've seen a plethora of TV programs about small quirky communities and seachangers. Then there are the reality TV shows about ethnic and regional cooking, satisfying our longing for fresh food that doesn't come plastic-wrapped from the supermarket.

Overarchingly, the treechange is being pushed along mainly by baby boomers, thought by many to be trying to recapture some of the values they espoused as hippies in the 1960s. They're cashed up and with the kids off their hands, pretty well free to live where they want.

It's a situation that appeals to state governments, especially in Victoria, NSW and Queensland, where population growth in the capital cities and along the coasts is a major headache. Victoria was first off the block in establishing incentives for people to quit Melbourne for a regional town. The campaign has been very successful. NSW has taken a more fragmented approach, with the regions themselves touting for new residents; now many of its regional centres are being dubbed renaissance towns. In Queensland, where the south-east corner is straining under the pressure of 1500 people arriving each week, the government has started looking to the country to solve its housing problems.

The growth is still patchy and some states are doing better than others at regenerating rural areas, but the push for the bush is now safely regarded as a long-term trend and no mere fad of a few disenchanted hippies.

Treechangers come from all age groups and walks of life. Even though the intention is probably much the same—escaping the urban madness for a better quality of life—they represent a significant, historic shift.

So, what is happening? Across Australia, about 100,000 people are leaving the cities annually for a new life by the sea or in the country. It's a figure that is growing at 7 per cent each year. Social commentator Bernard Salt recently found that about two million people or thereabouts would like to make the move but aren't sure how, and there is every chance they may join the exodus in the future. It is estimated conservatively that more than two million people will relocate in the coming decade.

This is a trend that has the business sector excited. New magazines are being formed, property developers are eyeing up land on the perimeters of country towns, and real estate agents are pitching their ads to treechangers. There's even a website called www.yourseachange.com devoted to helping people make the move out of suburbia. Local councils have been spurred on to develop new business plans and marketing programs. And to varying degrees and with differing results, state governments are getting behind the phenomenon and putting in place regional growth initiatives to capitalise on the social trend.

Downshifters are another group. These are people who accept less money through working fewer hours in order to have time for what they believe are the important things in life. It's often a quest for true happiness and fulfilment. Downshifters often also aim to consume less in order to reduce their ecological footprint. While seachangers and treechangers tend to be people in older age groups, downshifters include families with young children.

For the past decade or more, the focus has been squarely on the beach. The term seachangers was first coined to describe the thousands of people moving to the coast for a lifestyle close to the beach. ABC radio south-west program host, Steve Martin, believes he first coined the word treechange as the rural, non-coastal version of seachange, although he admits he saw treechange used in conjunction with a real estate advertisement in the Ballarat region.

Treechangers are taking over from seachangers. The now-entrenched social shift to the beach means Australia has seen the suburbanisation of its coastline. Skyrocketing beach-side property prices and city-like social and overcrowding problems have started to take their toll. As Australia's beachfront is progressively captured by the wealthy and the noisy, would-be lifestyle changers are modifying their aspirations. They are making a 180 degree turn and looking inland for their urban escape.

The trend towards rural living isn't confined to Australia. In countries like the USA and the UK, the flight from the urban sprawl is long established: in parts of North America, treechangers are called porchers because they want to have time to sit on the

Farmers' markets, such as this rural one in Talbot, Victoria, have given a new lease on life to small country towns, along with delis, provedores, wineries and boutique bakeries (photo: Neil Newitt). **Overleaf:** a quintessential Australian image from 1981—Doug Anthony, Deputy Prime Minister, regularly helped run the nation from his caravan in the northern NSW town of New Brighton during the summer holidays.

porch and yarn; in the UK, urbanites have been moving into country villages for a couple of decades or more. Now they are buying up homes and farms in regions of rural France and Italy dubbed 'Chianti-shire'.

Mirroring the rural shift is a proliferation of farmers' markets. In England, virtually every large country town has one of these and they are starting to take business share away from the increasingly concerned big supermarket chains as consumers express a desire to buy local and put their money into the pockets of their district growers.

Here in Australia, we're feeling the same pressures. We're retreating from the big issues thrown up by an increasingly globalised world and we're turning inwards for comfort and security. In what the social pundits call cocooning, we're focusing on local, more immediate and personal agendas over which we feel we can have some control.

Paradoxically, as many aspects of life become more global we yearn for the domestic and focus more on home and hearth. Every night, as TV news brings the horror of war and terrorism bang into the middle of our living rooms, we turn over and tune into programs about renovating our homes and backyards. We learn what not to wear, or how to improve our relationships. We take comfort in watching myriad cooking shows.

We are concerned that our sense of Australianness is being diluted. The coffee shop on the corner is one of a multinational chain. We are more likely to watch American TV drama than Australian-made programs. Our children use words and phrases borrowed from Beverly Hills or Chicago in preference to the dinky-di Aussie slang of their parents and grandparents.

These days, we are less confident about long-term relationships. We're anxious that the breakdown of community is reducing our sense of personal morality. Many of us are worried about job security and about having enough super for retirement. Some people are giving up the idea of retiring at 60 and are staying in the workforce longer. We're more likely to work part-time, have multiple jobs, work from home, or be running a small business. Yet it is Australia's strong financial position, together with record city property values, that have enabled more of us to be able to afford to sell up and make a move while still feeling financially secure.

Put it down to anti-globalism or a nostalgic bid for a return to community life. But ask any treechanger why they've made the move and they'll give you much the same set of answers.

Primarily, it's about reducing stress and pressure in their lives. They are fed up with working long hours—Australians work more hours per week than residents of any other OECD country. They want to get away from the seemingly endless traffic queues and the time squandered commuting to work—a 19-minute daily drive adds up to two weeks of extra work each year. They want 'out' of the dead end jobs and the high rise office blocks.

They want to have more time to themselves and their families, find a sense of community which they believe no longer exists in the cities, and have more security for their kids. They are sick and tired of the urban sprawl, the monotony of the suburbs, and the loss of identity of the neighbourhoods.

Many want to change their source of income, take on other less demanding work, or be more autonomous and become self-employed. Some want to go onto the land and become self-sustaining. The majority say they want to be more in touch with themselves and their environment. The reality is that although Australians are generally wealthier than ever before, many believe they are no happier.

Demographic research dispels the popular notion that it is retirees who are opting out. Most urban escapees are in their 40s, 50s and 60s—the baby boomers. They've watched the value of their capital city home rise and rise. They've paid off the loan and they are cashing in. They can buy a place in a country town with enough left over to live on. They are swapping office jobs for part-time less stressful work. They are starting new country town businesses, buying shops or going into the B&B trade.

More recently, they have found themselves joined by a growing number of younger people. These are aged between 35 and 40 and have young families. Rural councils like them. They are more flexible, less demanding than their baby boomer counterparts and they are more likely to start new businesses than to buy existing ones. Unlike the older baby boomer, they are also less cashed up and therefore less prone to paying over the odds for property, thereby pushing up the prices beyond the reach of the locals.

For the existing country communities, treechangers can be a mixed blessing. The influx of newbies means a greater diversity of people with new ideas and often higher expectations. This is exciting for the locals—but challenging. The increase in population is generating new business and employment opportunities but it is also creating a few problems.

The arrival of retirees and non-working treechangers is leading to a bigger demand for services and many towns just can't keep up. Many regional centres are battling a chronic shortage of skilled workers such as medical and teaching staff.

If you thought that the country was populated by people working on farms and pastoral properties, think again. These days, the number of people working directly in agriculture has fallen to 240,000 people or just 6.5 per cent of the rural working population. 78 per cent, or almost 2.9 million people, work in the service industries in the towns.

In towns across Australia, it is industries such as retail, health and education that are expected to dominate in the future.

Growing populations also mean that rural councils have to provide new infrastructure and services. A typical complaint from council is: "They come here to drop out and then they want all the services they have left behind in the city." In many places, the councils are being caught on the hop.

This is especially the case when it comes to maintaining housing affordability for country town locals. A shortage of housing means inevitably that property prices and rents will rise. As the developers move into town, they bring a completely new set of problems. Council planning departments and facilities become overstretched, the rural landscape is diminished and the area is in danger of losing the very qualities that once attracted people in the first place. Being able to balance all this is a skill many small town councillors just don't have, because they don't have the experience. The threat of suburbanisation is starting to bite and is dividing the living spaces, and the locals' opinions, within many country towns.

So where are people moving to? The treechange phenomenon occurs wherever there are attractive regional towns not too far from a major city. About 78 per cent of people relocate within their home state and most are living within a four-hour drive from a state capital or large population centre.

Tasmania, with its appealing architecture and low property prices, has long been luring treechangers—and they've been moving there from all parts of Australia. Pretty well all of Tassie can be regarded as treechange territory. They go to places such as Strahan, Penguin, St Helens, Shearwater, Ross, Oatlands and Campbell Town. In South Australia, the Adelaide Hills are a hot spot—towns such as Mount Barker have emerged as star performers. The Murray region and the Fleurieu Peninsula are also popular with treechangers.

For 20 years, south-east Queensland has been the fastest growing urban area in Australia, with the focus firmly on Brisbane and the beaches of the Gold and Sunshine coasts. But now the coastal hinterlands are beckoning urban escapees. The historic township of Boonah, 50 minutes drive south-west of Brisbane, is suddenly hip and happening and the latte set is buying country homes. Property prices have almost doubled in recent years. Toowoomba, high on the Dividing Range an hour and 20 minute drive west of Brisbane, has long lured retirees and baby boomers, but now, other big towns like Warwick are finding themselves attracting treechangers. The Marburg, Laidley and Gatton area just west of Brisbane has been 'discovered'. The wine growing area around Stanhope and the Granite Belt and the South Burnett are also on the treechange map.

Sydney treechangers are widespread throughout NSW. They can be found on hobby farms and wineries, and running businesses or behind the counters of cafes, craft centres and shops in towns stretching from Cooma, Jindabyne and Adaminaby in the Snowies, to Lismore, Tenterfield and Armidale in the north.

The Blue Mountains and the Southern Highlands have long been popular as have the Central Coast and the Hawkesbury. The outskirts of the ACT are also on the list along with Murrumbateman, Braidwood, Bungendore and Berridale. Singleton and the Hunter Valley are popular. Oberon, Dubbo, Tamworth, Bathurst, Orange and Young are also emerging as hot spots.

The NSW government holds Country Week each August to help sell the regions. It attracts crowds of 8000 to 10,000. The state has 13 regional development boards.

By far the greatest exodus to the bush has been in Victoria. It all began in the late 1990s when the then newly elected Premier, Steve Bracks, introduced programs to reverse the state's rural decline. No government has been more proactive in promoting regional development. Touted as introducing a new era for provincial Victoria, the programs have been phenomenally successful. By 2005, country Victoria's population was growing faster than Melbourne's. In the same period, the number of building approvals had more than doubled and more than 80,000 new jobs were created. Investment reached record highs with more than 300 new projects in country areas worth more than $5.4 billion.

Labelled lifestyle regions, the north-eastern part of the state and the Hume corridor—Mitchell, Strathbogie and Benalla—have been the focus of major growth and to a lesser extent, the towns along the Murray River and central Victoria. By 2030, provincial Victoria's population is forecast to grow by 350,000—more than the combined populations of Ballarat, Bendigo and Geelong.

The push to the country is inextricably linked with growth in regional tourism—and especially the increasing interest in the food and wine industries which has led to a revitalisation of many country areas. Regions such as Western Australia's Margaret River, Tasmania's north-eastern coast and Queensland's Sunshine Coast hinterland are seeing a big increase in small farmers producing niche foods. Places like Dubbo and Young are being tagged renaissance towns for their cafe cultures and the sort of innovative little eateries you'd normally only expect to see in an inner city.

Former city types are successfully growing and making foodstuffs to service the higher end deli market and their passionate approaches to their crafts are paying dividends. They are keeping goats and making cheeses and ice-cream; they are growing niche fruits, vegetables and herbs; and they are manufacturing items such as spices and condiments. They are showing themselves keen to take up new technologies and search for better ways. They are having a positive influence on animal husbandry, often treating the animals in their care like family pets in the belief that it makes for better milk, cheese—whatever.

Organics has become a big part of the scene. Australia has the largest amount of land in the world registered for organic production. Across broad areas of all states, you'll find organic tea, coffee, fruit and vegies—even organic wine, as well as meat production.

The food producers have spawned a tourist industry of farm-gate shops and pick-your-own produce. Foodie travellers in search of new tastes can now find delis and provedores in even the smallest towns.

Smart chefs have been lured away from the cities to country areas to establish new eateries and are creating new specifically regional cuisine based on local produce.

While the treechange phenomenon has focused on the rural areas of the south and within the broader coastal strip, the big influences on growth in the remote areas have been the resources boom—which has repopulated many Western Australian and Queensland inland towns—and the proliferation of outback tourism.

Tourism is proving vital for the financial wellbeing of isolated communities. A good example is the Queensland region of Carpentaria, one of Australia's most remote areas, around the towns of Karumba and Normanton. The Shire Council reports the tourism industry contributes $11 million a year to the local coffers, and indirectly $14.1 million, and that 16 per cent of the local population works in tourism or a tourism-related industry—that's three times the national average.

The inland travel scene includes two groups of people who are either long-term visitors or temporary residents, depending on your definition. They are at opposite ends of the age spectrum, and a generation or more apart: the backpackers and the grey nomads. The two groups are having a massive impact on the regional economy and the fact is that some small—and some not so small—communities are beginning to rely on the income generated by their presence.

Backpackers have been around since as far back as the late 1980s. They've grown in numbers until now an estimated half a million a year are on the road somewhere in

Tourism and the resulting influx of new residents, in the form of hard-working backpackers and enterprising treechangers, have significantly boosted the bush economy (photo: Wayne Taylor).

Australia. The majority of the internationals are from Europe with by far the greatest number coming from the UK. They are mostly aged between 20 and 24 with about 10 per cent between 24 and 29 and 8 per cent still in their teens.

While many stick to the coastline, serving in bars, cafes, resorts and dive shops as they go, an increasing number are working on farms and taking the country route. The more adventurous are doing jackarooing courses and heading outback.

Another group of new travellers in the country regions are the WWOOFERs—Willing Workers on Organic Farms. The movement is worldwide. It is a form of cultural exchange in which participants live and work as part of the family on host farms and learn about the skills of organic growing and the area they are visiting.

Most hosts are pursuing a simple, sustainable lifestyle. Many are permaculture enthusiasts, and about 20 per cent use biodynamic growing methods. About 25 per cent of the farms are commercial producers, whether full or part time. Some hosts are alternative, co-operative communities, and a few are communal living groups.

WWOOFERs work on a voluntary basis. They're in it for the experience. They usually get their bed and board provided. Often the job will be simple farm work, but it can also include environmental work such as tree planting for desalination, erosion control or wildlife habitat creation.

But by far the biggest impact is now coming from the 350,000 or so caravans, campervans and mobile homes on the road piloted by the intrepid grey nomads: the mainly baby boomers who are renting out the family home—or even selling it—and taking off on their long-dreamed-of around-Australia adventure.

Grey nomad expenditure adds over $2 billion to Australia's domestic economy annually, most of which is spent in regional Australia. An estimated 17,000 caravans are being sold annually and 80 per cent of these are being bought by people aged over 50. According to the nomads themselves, they are a phenomenon that is here to stay.

They are shunning suburbia and putting off overseas travel because of what they see on TV of Bali, London and New York. While some are prepared to rough it in modest caravans or even tents, by far the majority are taking their creature comforts with them and investing in top-of-the-range motor homes and four-wheel drives. Some are converting buses or even having their mobile home-away-from-home custom built. They have indoor toilets, showers, microwaves, fridges, washing machines, dryers, televisions, CD players, laptop computers—you name it.

Some grey nomads are on the road for a couple of months, others for a couple of years. And they are leading a gypsy lifestyle, supporting themselves with temporary work. They are helping to fill the labour shortages on the land by replacing the fruit pickers and farm workers who have been tempted away to the city or the mines. Many grey nomads are undertaking voluntary work, helping the communities they visit.

It's about getting away from the power bills, the rates, the insurance and all of the stuff associated with suburbia. But while many of them regard their travels as a prolonged holiday, others need to support themselves financially at least to some degree. It appears their energy and old-fashioned work ethic makes them sought-after employees. In the remoter regions they can be a godsend, doing jobs like gardening, cleaning and laundry. Nomads with trade skills, such as mechanics, carpenters or tilers, are in even greater demand, as are teachers and some other professionals.

No corner of the continent is left undiscovered, from the Bay of Fires in Tassie to the MacDonnell Ranges in the Northern Territory. In the winter months (the northern Australian dry season), caravan parks in the north are packed with nomads escaping the southern winter. They are now being joined by overseas baby boomers and retirees—in particular, Pommie nomads—in search of some sun.

They have been described as a significant but benign force. And they are not being overlooked by the business community. Their strength and expected longevity as a market force are amply displayed on www.thegraynomads.com.au, an on-line magazine for the nomad community. Produced by a couple who had already been on the road for more than a year when they launched the first issue, it provides useful advice for would-be nomads and inspirational features about those already out there. By and large, nomads are enthusiastic networkers and keep in touch with others in 'the club'. They communicate with each other by UHV radio, arranging where to meet up and letting everyone know what is coming next on the social timetable. Most are married couples—often travelling with the family pet—but it's not uncommon to find two women on the road together. Nomads generally live simply, keeping the household budget down to about $55 a day.

A problem for the nomads is the reduction in caravan parks across Australia as especially those in prime positions are being bought and developed for housing. It's a particular problem in Queensland. In Victoria, however, the state government responded by effectively abolishing land tax for caravan parks, encouraging owners not to sell.

Despite a few relatively minor issues, it would seem that nomads are by and large an optimistic lot—always keen to find out what's around the next bend and what the next stop has to offer. Once on the road, many find the lifestyle addictive and despite calls from anxious family and friends, put off going back home. There are early pioneering nomads who have been on the road for a decade or more. The freedom of the open road obviously offers something that resonates with many Australians.

So it looks like Australia is coming full circle. We're returning to the bush—but in new guises—and the future for the rural areas is starting to look very exciting. No previous generation has had such freedom of choice over where they will live. With enough financial stability and with 21st century technology and communications we can live and work just about anywhere and any way we want to. As treechangers, we can start a cheese farm, buy a winery or run a B&B in a food and wine region. Or we can run a consultancy from a computer and phone at home—and home can be anywhere. We can transfer our existing city job to a similar one in a regional town and with a lower mortgage and overheads, we can work as much or as little as we can get away with.

When we reach our fifties and sixties we can take to the open road as grey nomads. We can work a few hours a week and volunteer to do something that gives us the satisfaction of helping others. We now know that in the 21st century you don't need a fortune to lead a satisfying and rewarding life. Let the millionaires have their inner-city penthouses or their beachfront mansions: for most of us a yarn and a laugh is all we need at the end of the day. When you think about it, it's much the same sentiment that was expressed by the old bush poets.

Whichever way you look at it, the bush is being reshaped. In just a few years, technology has swept away much of the social isolation while groups like treechangers are taking the plunge by moving out of the city and changing the demographic make-up of the regions. So far, local residents appear welcoming of their city cousins, keen to have the income and the additional clout in state and federal governments that an expanded population base brings.

But the key to long-term success will depend on the pace of growth and how well the under-resourced small councils dotted around the regions cope with it. The potential for big subdivisions and supermarket giants will not be welcomed by all treechangers in search of a quiet life and the stage could be set for community battles. It represents a tough problem for councils who are increasingly finding themselves the meat in the sandwich between an unhappy electorate and companies who have the legal right to develop. Compensation can be costly. The answer lies with the state governments promoting decentralisation as part of their way of dealing with congested cities. Town planning could become the new regional employment opportunity in the years to come.

One thing is certain: while life in the bush might be taking on a range of new and different nuances, thanks largely to technology, those elusive natural qualities that so endear the bush to Australians are as vibrant and appealing as ever.

An increasingly more common picture of bush life—drovers have been joined by travelers in caravans on the outback roads, as seen here on the lonely Barkly Highway in remote Queensland (photo: Heath Missen).

THE
LA

ND

THE LAND

Robert Hughes describes Australia as the "utterly enigmatic continent", and that before Cook and Phillip arrived on its 'fatal' shore, it was: "locked in its historic immensity of blue heat, bush, sandstone and the measured booming of glassy Pacific rollers".

Many would argue that in essence, the land hasn't changed in 250 years. It's as tough and as unforgiving as ever, prone to heat, winds, floods and droughts and underlying it all, of course, the tyranny of distance.

Rural communities know all about natural Australia in its terrifying shapes and forms—storms that shoot down lightning bolts of fearsome wattage; bushfires that roar through at the speed of an express train, razing all in their path, leaving nothing but black stumps in their wake; unstoppable floods that swiftly engulf square kilometre after kilometre of the landscape; and, in between times, the slow life-draining horror of drought.

In the first few years of the Sydney Cove colony, the white population lived on the brink of starvation while they came to grips with farming in such an alien world. In the first 50 years, new settlers watched as explorers tramped off to open up further tracts of the continent—many, such as Burke and Wills, never to return. Heat and death were just a factor of life.

But throughout it all, they persevered. They built homes and towns, railways, mines and ports. By the 20th century, Australia's farming and mining sectors had made it rich beyond the most optimistic dreams of its forefathers. Granted, many romanticised the life of the pioneer and the settler, but it was also a life that carried a freedom not found in the 'old' world.

Communication then and now. Mail carried on horseback could take weeks to reach its recipient **(above)**. Although it doesn't extend far into the outback and reception can be patchy, mobile phones **(opposite left)** are a welcome addition for many farmers (photo: Sean Davey). Today, Australia Post deliveries can be conducted by air **(opposite right)**, speeding things up considerably, particularly for far-flung properties (photo: Steven Siewert).

The bush network

Until the first railway opened in 1854, horses, bullock drays and human foot were the only way to get around. From the 1820s, coaches were the main source of public transport; the first service ran from Sydney to Parramatta twice a day at the hefty cost of six shillings a ticket. The gold rush brought American prospectors to Victoria and three of them came up with an idea for a coach service along the lines of Wells Fargo. They started Cobb & Co, which was to become the lifeline of communities in Victoria, New South Wales and Queensland.

Given its isolation, it's no surprise that Australia has a long history of enthusiasm for communication technology. It started with the first telephone system linking Melbourne and south Melbourne in 1879—records show that 7757 calls were made in 1884—and it has continued right up to today with the internet and satellite technology, which has transformed life in the bush.

AUSTRALIAN BUSH LIFE—MUSTERING CATTLE.—[SEE PAGE 4.]

CAMEL WAGGON CONVEYING PRISONERS AND PATIENTS FROM MOUNT BROWNE.

Before cars, the rough Australian landscape ensured that transport by four-legged animal became priceless. A 19th-century sketch of a muster **(above)**, with the captured wild horses later broken for riding. Camels were used instead of horses by Cobb & Co. during the drought of the 1880s **(right)**. Rough journeys in carts drawn by oxen **(opposite)** were common in the 1850s.

MOUNT VICTORIA PASS NSW

The early settlers constructed roads and bridges with vigour, opening up the land to settlement and trade. A small locomotive hauls logs across a timber trestle bridge **(above)**, typical of the type constructed in 1900 in NSW. Carts on the Mount Victoria Pass to Hartley and Bathurst, NSW, in 1887 **(opposite)**.

IMMARNA

To cross the country's vast distances, we've employed all means of transport, with the extensive railway service being the most enduring and romanticised. For the more heavily populated bush regions, regular passenger services were viable, such as the 'express' locomotive **(left)** that ran between Sydney and Albury, trialled in January 1943 (photo: E.C. Bowen), and the Comet **(above)** that ran between Broken Hill and Parkes, which started in 1937 and was championed as the first airconditioned service in the country (photo: Peter Morrison). A 1924 image of Immarna **(opposite)** on the Trans Australia Rail Route (photo: H.H. Fishwick).

Big industry requires big transport options. With the completion of the Ghan train line in 2003 **(above)**, cargo can easily be taken from Adelaide up to the port of Darwin for export to Asia and beyond; this photo shows the inaugural freight train on January 16, 2004. Huge road trains **(opposite)** are the unique Aussie solution to moving large quantities of freight (photos: David Moir).

ROAD TRAINS
53·5 METRES LONG

The town

From the Victorian high country to the red centre, the bush town in its various shapes and forms is embedded in the Australian psyche. However, in some areas they are an endangered species, slowly vanishing from the landscape as family farms are amalgamated to form big corporate enterprises and the local populations that support them dwindle. This has created a growing divide: while many of the larger country towns are getting bigger, smaller places are disappearing altogether. There are the exceptions. In areas closer to the city and coast, some towns are receiving a new lease on life thanks to tourism and treechangers. Dubbed 'renaissance towns', they boast many of the cultural attributes normally associated with the city, such as shopping and cafes, as well as those other earthly delights—a circle of friends, good food and wine, and a laid-back lifestyle.

With Charles Rasp's discovery of silver and lead in 1883, soon followed by the arrival of a tramway, Broken Hill grew quickly, but its expansion has slowed somewhat with the decline of the mining industry. An early image of the town's main street **(above left)**, date unknown (photo: Peter Morris, taken from the original); the same street today **(above right)**—note the communications tower above the Post Office in the background (photo: Jessica Shapiro); and the bustling main street in 1944 **(opposite)**.

W. HADAD & SONS
WICKS
BROADWAY CAFE
MARTINS
the Jeweller
COX BROS
COX BROS

GARDINERS

Named in honour of the Dutch prince, William of Orange, the town of Orange in New South Wales first appeared on a map in 1829, and became an important trading centre with the discovery of gold at Ophir in 1851 and, later, at other nearby towns. Summer Street, looking west, in the early 1900s **(above left)**; the same street in 1948 **(opposite)**, showing Western Stores on the left; by 2004 **(above right)** the roads are looking much more congested (photo: Peter Morris).

The homestead

The Australian country homestead is the bush dweller's castle, and a measure of success, status and family history. Far from the sprawling residences of today, the first settlers' homes were simple slab huts with earth floors. One-roomed timber cottages were built—often with a lean-to—and more rooms were added as the owners became financially secure and children were born. When Australia grew wealthy from its gold and wool booms in the mid- to late-19th century, the pastoral dynasties and the resources tycoons threw themselves into building ever grander mansions to reflect their new-found stature.

The architecture of Australia is as varied as the climate. In the first 100 years of settlement, most styles were borrowed from Britain and introduced by migrant architects and craftsmen, in particular colonial, Victorian and gothic designs. Weatherboard and corrugated iron were the most popular materials. Australia was blessed with outstanding hard woods for joinery and lightweight tin could be easily manufactured and transported to construct roofs and even walls. Today, each state displays a distinctive style. In Tasmania and South Australia the early settlers built elegant homesteads out of solid sandstone to withstand the freezing winters. In Queensland, they opted for timber and tin and built their houses high on stilts to help keep them cool during the summer heatwaves.

Whatever its appearance, the homestead is a haven, a retreat from the elements, the backbreaking work and the endless expanse of country that surrounds it.

With people leaving the land due to drought and corporations buying up what were once separate propeties, many thriving family homes have been left to rot. A sad image of an abandoned farm near Deniliquin, NSW (photo: Louie Douvis).

This glass negative **(opposite)** gives an idyllic image of a well-kept bush property in the early 20th century (photo: H.H. Fishwick). For many, their homestead contains too many memories, too much of their lives, for them to ever want to leave. This Ensay farmer pictured in 2000 **(above)**, sold all but his house in a government buy-back scheme (photo: Jason South). Despite financial troubles, this farmer **(left)** battled to stay on his Taree farm in 2001 (photo: Stefan Moore).

Arresting and timeless, images of drought speak volumes. This drawing by Russell Drysdale **(above)** dates from December 1944, when he and reporter Keith Newman journeyed to Wentworth to report on what was then the worst drought in memory: "one long tragedy-track over scorched earth". In March 1998 Steve Arbuthnot **(opposite)** was pictured walking under the bridge that spanned a nonexistent Lake Eildon near his home town of Bonnie Doon, Victoria (photo: Simon O'Dwyer).

The droughts

Drought is an immutable fact of Australian life. It is arguably nature's cruellest force: not the instant bang of a storm or cyclone, but instead the agonisingly long draining of life from the land, along with the animals and humans who live on it. The early farmers and pastoralists soon learnt that dry spells could last for years.

> *The drought came down on the field and flock,*
> *And never a raindrop fell,*
> *Though the tortured moans of the starving stock*
> *Might soften a fiend from hell.*
>
> 'The Swagman'—A.B. 'Banjo' Paterson

The search for water was a constant theme in Captain James Cook's journals, and many of Australia's inland explorers perished through lack of it. Rainfall figures show that out of every 10 years we have about three good years, four average, and three bad. Severe drought affects some part of Australia about once every 18 years.

Severe droughts produce alien images. Two residents of Broken Hill **(opposite)** during the water shortage of December 1944. Ray Canny **(above left and right)** must be all too aware that history can repeat itself. In the first of these photos taken at Woorinen, Victoria, he feeds stock from the back of a ute during the 1982 drought. The second image shows him at the same place, this time in 2002 (photo: John Woudstra).

The floods

The pastoralists of the Gulf and Channel country of Far North Queensland depend on the floods that cover kilometre after kilometre during the annual wet season, seeping their way across vast tracts of the continent—areas the size of entire European countries. It's then that the country comes to life; flowers that haven't blossomed for a year burst into bloom and the lush plains of Mitchell grass, that feed the big Brahman herds, spring new growth.

It is flash flooding that presents the real danger. Flash floods strike terror into the hearts of the farmers of New South Wales and Victoria, and typically come in the wake of slow-moving lows and big tropical thunderstorms—systems that can drop vast amounts of water in a very short time. The strong updrafts inside these storms suspend huge quantities of rain before releasing a deluge from the sky at rates of more than 10 centimetres an hour. Residents of bush towns have learnt to live with the prospect of evacuation and many travellers are caught unawares by swiftly swollen rivers and submerged roads.

Australians are a resourceful lot. A teenager 'rides' through streets that have become rivers **(above)**. A cup of tea fortifies a resident **(opposite)** as she cleans up after the June 1949 floods that hit Maitland. **Overleaf:** rowboats in the bush aren't such a strange idea—in May 1962 they saved the day at Raymond Terrace, Maitland (photo: A. Kemp); and when cars get bogged there's always walking, as these people were forced to do on the Hume Highway near Wagga Wagga in July 1956 (photo: A. Iverson).

Peters
ICE CREAM
LAN-CHOO TEA
LF B2611

The flood waters rise around a lone farmhouse **(left)** near Wangaratta, Victoria, in September 1996 (photo: Sebastian Costanzo). And when the waters disperse, that's when the real work begins: Bill and Harold Batty **(above)** repair some of the 3 kilometres of damaged fencing on a Swift Creek property, Victoria, in July 1998 (photo: Craig Sillitoe).

It will be remembered as one of the worst bushfires in Australia's history. Watching the hills burn **(above)** on infamous Ash Wednesday, 1983. A common summer sight **(opposite)**: the fire danger is extreme in Royal National Park, NSW, in December 1979. **Overleaf:** sometimes, you stand and fight—the exhausted Mrs Keene washes her eyes after defending her home in Engadine, NSW; a thirsty firefighter from 1950.

The fires

Each summer, most of the southern parts of Australia brace themselves for the bushfire season, simply a part of life. The daily weather forecast on television delivers the bushfire risk, and the fire brigade stands at the ready. New South Wales, Victoria, South Australia and Tasmania are some of the most fire-prone regions in the world. Often, the huge fires are sparked by lightning strikes from seasonal storms, or accidents with powerlines or farm machinery. Sometimes they are deliberately lit by arsonists. They can develop on several fronts at a time, fanned by strong wind, and when they get going there's little that can stop them. People who live in these areas ready themselves as best they can but the sheer force and unpredictability of the fires means that lives and homes are often lost. The 1983 Ash Wednesday fires in Victoria and South Australia went down as some of the worst in history, when 2500 homes were lost, 450,000 hectares destroyed and 25 people killed.

The cost of fires, of course, can be devastating. The Golden Age Hotel in Day Street, Omeo, Victoria **(above)**, was totally destroyed in 1939. A silent killer: the 'Ignition Tree' **(right)**, a red stringy bark in Brindabella National Park, west of Canberra, starts to regrow one year after it was struck by lightning, igniting the McIntyre's Hut Fire of early 2003, which caused four deaths and more than 500 houses to be destroyed (photo: Andrew Taylor). Driving towards danger **(opposite top)**: a dramatic sight as plumes of smoke billow over the Newell Highway, north of Parkes, on 30 November, 2004 (photo: Dallas Kilponen). Elvis the helitanker **(opposite bottom)** flies to the rescue over Macquarie Park in the fires of Christmas 2001 (photo: Nick Moir).

The human spirit—and the human cost. Australians carry on 'til stumps, as do these cricketers **(above)** in Cessnock, NSW, in October 2002 (photo: Darren Pateman). A grazier **(opposite top)** feels the pain of having to shoot his cattle after fires swept through the Alpine Region, Victoria, in January 2003 (photo: Simon O'Dwyer). With some fires there's no choice but to run—a child hugs her teddy bear **(opposite bottom)** as she's evacuated from Sandy Point, across the Georges River, NSW, in December 2002 (photo: Andrew Meares).

The natural balance

Australia's ecosystem is vulnerable to pests because its native plants and animals were isolated for many millions of years and they can put up little resistance to new species, almost all introduced since European settlement. Our best known pests are the rabbits and cane toads, but the continent has a long list of unwanteds—both flora and fauna. Dingoes were probably the first animal to be introduced and, in the early days of settlement, foxes. But the list also includes many domesticated species turned wild—pigs, camels, goats, horses, dogs and cats. Not only are these animals in competition with domesticated stock for food, they eat crops and destroy the natural environment. Wild pigs are a major source of tuberculosis in the north and west. Dogs that were once family pets are a threat to livestock, hunting in packs to bring down cattle and sheep. Weeds such as lantana are choking the life out of Australia's forests while river pests such as water hyacinth are clogging the waterways.

Nature's punishment for our meddling can sometimes reach Biblical proportions. Prickly pear **(above)** was introduced in the early 1800s as stock fodder and simply to liven up the garden, but it thrived too well and ended up colonising huge swathes of the country—by 1952 it covered 62 million acres in NSW and Queensland and forced people off their farms; it was finally conquered by another introduced species, the cactoblastis caterpillar. Serious outbreaks of the Australian plague locust **(opposite)** occur about every two years, following successive seasons of good rainfall—this photo was taken at Dubbo in March 2004.

Little did we know what havoc could be caused by simple actions. Thomas Austin released 24 rabbits on his property near Geelong, Victoria, in 1859 so he could hunt them for sport; by 1941, when this picture of a man putting a ferret down a hole was taken **(opposite)**, farmers were desperate to be rid of the pests. Erected in the 1880s, The Dog Fence **(above)** is the longest in the world and was intended to protect the sheep stocks of the south-east from dingoes; it was only partially successful, as some did get through, and the lack of predators allowed rabbit and kangaroo populations to flourish (photo: Steven Siewert).

By introducing species and occupying land, we've seriously affected animal populations; our challenge now is to keep numbers at a sustainable level. Despite our affection for them in national culture, brumbies **(above left)** are incompatible with fragile ecosystems (photo: Dallas Kilponen). With kangaroo numbers estimated at about 50 million **(above right)**, government-managed culling is intended to protect the environment (photo: Andrew Meares). Koalas **(opposite)** have been successfully protected—so successfully, in fact, that there are now too many of them to survive on the available resources (photo: Damian White).

THE WO

RK

THE WORK

Ask just about anyone on the land what draws them to the job and they'll tell you it's the lifestyle. In an age when the city offers good pay and steady incomes, there are still plenty of young people who want to make a life for themselves on the land.

For many it's the chance to work with animals—especially horses. They're central to the lifestyle and play a huge role in attracting new people to the bush and keeping them there. In the bush, everyone is passionate about horses and social life revolves around them, whether it be horseracing, polocrosse or that most beloved of Australian sports, camp drafting.

For others, it's the sense of freedom they get from an outdoor rural life—whether its droving, wheat farming, timberwork or protecting the bush as a national park ranger. It's something they just can't find behind an office desk. This is not a new phenomenon. Back in the days of Henry Lawson and A.B. 'Banjo' Paterson, they knew they were writing for an audience more at home in an office chair than a saddle, but yearning for the other. Just think of Paterson's most famous lines about swapping places with Clancy:

And the hurrying people daunt me, and their pallid faces haunt me
As they shoulder one another in their rush and nervous haste,
With their eager eyes and greedy, and their stunted forms and weedy,
For townsfolk have no time to grow, they have no time to waste.

And I somehow rather fancy that I'd like to change with Clancy,
Like to take a turn at droving where the seasons come and go,
While he faced the round eternal of the cash-book and the journal—
But I doubt he'd suit the office, Clancy, of "The Overflow".

In many ways, working on the land today is as physically hard as it was 150 years ago—rising before dawn, finishing after sunset, dealing with obstreperous cattle or complicated machinery. There are some things that technology just can't change. But the people who live in the bush know better than most that you have to take the rough with the smooth if you want to get the best out of life.

The logging

The timber industry started within days of the First Fleet's arrival at Sydney Cove when trees were felled for housing and sawpits, powered by convicts, were erected. It was hard manual work. The free settlers brought water-powered sawmills and a little later, steam engines. The first logs were carried on the shoulders of a convict 'centipede'. Soon, bullocks replaced manpower and eventually, draught horses were introduced. Tramways were built into the forests to take timber to the nearest coast as it could be moved around more easily by boat. In the early days, land transport was 20 times more expensive than by water.

There was little control over how much was felled, with the result that vast tracts of timber were cleared with only the best trees selected, and much wasted. It wasn't until the 1890s that people recognised the need for conservancy. Timber was cut under government licence. From the 1890s to the 1940s the industry was dominated by small family firms. Many were backed by big city timber merchants who guaranteed an income by taking a portion of their output.

A George Bell image of timbergetters **(opposite)** at work with their axes in 1910. Conservationists **(left)** make a brave stand against the overwhelming might of big business (photo: Andrew De La Rue).

Without the benefit of machine-powered tools, mighty trees had to be cut into manageable sections by hand **(opposite)**; these champion cross-cut sawmen, Charlie Winkle and Bill Stewart, are pictured in the Atherton Tablelands in 1929 (photo: H.H. Fishwick). A feller in the Styx Valley in Tasmania **(above)** shows how the work is slightly easier, though no less hazardous, today (photo: Steven Siewert).

Though less romantic than ox-drawn wagons **(opposite)**, captured in NSW and Queensland in 1929 by H.H. Fishwick, the giant logging trucks **(above)** that thunder along bush roads have practical pulling power; this one is pictured in East Gippsland in 2004 (photo: Sandy Scheltema).

The farming

From an inauspicious start which saw the Sydney Cove colony reach starvation point many times in the first few years, Australia has grown to become one of the world's major food exporters.

In the early days it was just a matter of feeding the small colony by growing wheat and grazing sheep but, within a decade, huge tracts of land were being cleared and pastures opened up. The advent of the railways in the 1850s and 1860s gave farmers access to some of the more remote areas, cities and ports.

The generally dry climate and poorer soils in many areas were a challenge to the settlers more used to European conditions and methods. Irrigation systems were eventually developed throughout parts of Victoria and New South Wales.

By Federation, Australia was producing beef and dairy cattle and a wide range of grain, fruit and vegetable crops. Western Australia became a major grain producer. Queensland built an industry around sugar cane and parts of South Australia, Victoria and New South Wales were growing grapes.

The two world wars and the depression took their toll on the farming sector, but the industry continued to grow with the help of government support and tariffs on imports.

While since the war, the relative importance of farming to the Australian economy has decreased, it is still a major force, generating about $39 billion gross value annually.

Although farms take up about 60 per cent of all land in Australia, only about three per cent of the population is employed directly in farming—about 370,000 people. Sadly, many of the small family farms have gone—the land amalgamated to create economically-efficient properties run by large corporations.

The power of the horse: pulling the plough in 1923, in Uki near Murwillumbah (photo: H.H. Fishwick).

H.V.McKAY PTY LTD SUNSHINE

The introduction of machinery provided some help to farm workers **(opposite)**; but, as this wheat lumper at Boggabri in 1933 shows **(above)**, the labour was often still back-breaking (photos: H.H. Fishwick).

Some things don't change all that much. Fruit-picking in 1933 **(above)** looks much the same as it does today. Now done with machinery, the harvesting of sugar cane **(opposite)** in North Queensland in 1929 was—and still is, despite the new technology—hot work (photo: H.H. Fishwick).

Then and now: a farmhand uses McKay's Harvesting Machinery to fill basic grain bags **(above)**, in H.H. Fishwick's 1933 image. Now, of course, men are dwarfed by farming machinery **(opposite top)** and fewer people are needed to work the land (photo: Joe Armao). An imposing line-up of grain silos **(opposite bottom)** stores the precious harvest (photo: Simon O'Dwyer).

2188
CASE

Heading in new directions. These farmers **(above)**, pictured in September 1999, have a 750-acre organic farm on the Jenolan Caves Road near the Blue Mountains, NSW (photo: Robert Pearce). A May 2005 photo **(opposite)** shows a farmer with some of his 17,000 free-range chooks—they have 50 acres in which to roam (photo: Simon O'Dwyer).

An old gold digger **(above)** relies on the ingenuity of his windlass in 1908—an image by George Bell. A defunct mine head **(opposite)** makes for a beautiful sunset in Broken Hill, NSW (photo: Rick Stevens).

The mining

Australia's rich natural resources have underpinned its economy. Coal was its very first export commodity. Lieutenant John Shortland RN stumbled across it in 1797 when he was actually searching for escaped convicts near Newcastle. The coal was of such a high quality that, in 1801, 24 tons was loaded onto the schooner *Francis* and sent back to Sydney. Within a few months the coal was being sold overseas.

The first metal mined in Australia was lead at Glen Osmond, South Australia, in 1841 and within a decade, exports of copper and lead from South Australia alone earned more than Australia's combined exports of wool and wheat.

But gold was the big one. The first reported findings came in 1823 from surveyor James McBrien working near Bathurst. Nothing much happened until seasoned prospector Edward Hargraves set out to prove that Australia's geological features were perfect for gold; the government declared a gold discovery in May 1851. Prospectors cancelled their passages to California; labourers, office workers and servants unanimously threw in their jobs and headed west. The first Australian gold rush was on! Thousands came from overseas and the national economy was transformed overnight. By the 1850s, Australia was producing almost 40 per cent of the world's gold.

An exquisite glass negative of the Glen Greta mine near Maitland, NSW **(above)**. At the beginning of the 20th century the mining town of Joadja Creek, NSW **(opposite)**, produced kerosene, oil and candles; the only way into the town was on the hair-raising railway line, which ran down a 45-degree slope.

Gold prospectors, photographed by George Bell in 1910.

The many faces of the Aussie miner. Living conditions were basic and competition may have been fierce, but mateship was very much in evidence during the Newport gold discovery of 1930 **(opposite)**. Doing the ironing underground at Coober Pedy, SA **(above)**, where men defy the heat in search of opals (photo: Julian Kingma). Zinc miners at work in Broken Hill, NSW, photographed in October 1941 **(left)**.

The sheep

Most famously, Australia was said to be 'riding on the sheep's back' because, for decades, wool was the cornerstone of its agriculture and economy.

The first sheep to arrive in Australia were fat-tailed sheep from the Cape of Good Hope. They were on board the First Fleet as a food source and it wasn't until 1797 when John Macarthur and the Reverend Samuel Marsden brought in the first Spanish merinos—famous for their fine wool—to start a breeding program that the focus shifted to wool rather than meat.

The first auction of Australian wool was held 24 years later at Garraway's Coffee House in London. By 1838, the annual wool clip was more than two million kilos. It was worth ten, or even as much as 20, times as much per ton as wheat. As a result, many of the early squatters found themselves wealthy almost overnight. They built big homesteads and established pastoral dynasties. Their wealth from wool prompted others to challenge their squatting rights and by 1861 leasehold systems were established. The 1870s and 1880s saw a huge expansion in the industry but the 1890s brought the ill-fated combination of lower wool prices and a prolonged drought that lasted well beyond federation year. Sheep numbers fell to almost half of their peak of 106 million.

In 1890 the shearers' strike sparked violent confrontation between the workers and pastoralists. The shearers, seeking better conditions and pay, formed into unions which merged in 1894 to form the Australian Workers' Union and also played a role in the subsequent emergence of the Australian Labour Party.

Wool enjoyed some of its best years during the 1920s and 1930s, but it was during the 1950s that it saw its boom years as demand returned after World War II.

An H.H. Fishwick image of women inspecting wool at the Sydney ram sales, in 1936.

Sorting in the woolshed **(opposite)**. The shearer's job is for life **(above)**, and spans the generations; these workers are pictured at Corynnia station near Carrathool, NSW (photos: Kate Geraghty).

This photo from the 1930s **(opposite)** shows a young shearer who looks remarkably contemporary. Still doing it the traditional way **(left)**: shearers at work in Mangalore, Victoria, in 1999 (photo: Joe Armao). But are the days of the shearer at an end? In 1998, Bioclip introduced a method which enables the wool to be peeled from a sheep's back **(above)** with the aid of a protein injection and a netted vest; it's now used commercially on tens of thousands of young sheep (photo: Andrew Taylor).

Before and after: glass negatives showing sheep yarded for shearing **(above)** at Boonoke station, NSW, and wool bales **(opposite)** arriving at Jerilderie railway yards near Boonoke station (photos: H.H. Fishwick).

Mr H.L. Austin **(above)**, eminent sheep breeder for the 'Eli Elwah' station at Hay, NSW, in a photo by H.H. Fishwick. Inspecting the wool at the Sydney ram sales in 1931, also by Fishwick **(opposite)**.

CHARLES MILLS
UARDRY
NZL

No longer do the shears go 'click', but you still need to keep your equipment in good order **(opposite)**: oiling the tools (photo: Stefan Moore). Charlie Prell **(above)** yards some of his stud Corridales for shearing on Gundowringa near Crookwell, NSW; the family have been on the property since 1904 (photo: Peter Morris). **Overleaf:** a rare moment for quiet contemplation (photo: Peter Stoop).

The cattle

You could say that the Australian cattle industry started in January 1788 with two bulls and 11 cows, which arrived with the First Fleet. For a prison colony that would struggle to survive its first few years, cattle were critical both for milk and meat, and each successive ship would carry new stock.

The cattle industry grew fast with the first Shorthorns imported in 1825 and Herefords in 1826. They were the dominant breeds in the early days. There were the occasional introductions of Bos Indicus from India but there were no consistent importation and breeding programs until the 1930s when the Waverly Cattle Stud imported Brahmans from the USA.

It wasn't long before the pioneer cattlemen pushed north and west into Queensland, the Northern Territory and the Kimberley region of Western Australia. The Australian population growth of the 1840s and 1850s meant that demand for meat kept increasing and the herd grew in line with demand. The gold rushes pushed up demand even further. In 1872, the miners in Charters Towers, Queensland, tied ropes to the butcher's shop and pulled it down in protest over meat prices. But meat was cheap here in comparison with prices overseas. Visitors to Australia often commented on the fact that people could eat meat three times a day.

Mutton had been the Australian staple since the colony was founded but by the 1890s, beef overtook mutton as the preferred choice. In 1890, the average Australian (including babies) ate one third of a kilo of meat daily. In Queensland, it was half a kilo of meat each day—twice as much as the average Englishman and American and 12 times as much as the average Italian.

Australia's first export market was Britain—starting from the middle of the 19th century. But it wasn't until 1880 with a world-first shipment of frozen beef carcases from Sydney to London that a large-scale beef export industry was established.

Rounding up the herd at Cobungra, one of the largest cattle stations in Victoria (photo: John Lamb).

Online auctions, which reduce freight costs and the risks to stock, may see the end of saleyard scenes. The men at this undated auction **(opposite)** seem formally dressed in their suits and ties. The Akubra is still in evidence, though, at this 1998 auction **(above)** in the Bairnsdale Saleyards (photo: John Donegan).

Yesterday's dairy workers wouldn't recognise the industry today. A girl milks by hand **(opposite)** in the 1930s, while this rotary dairy **(above)** pictured in November 1999 near Swan Hill, Victoria, can milk 1360 cows twice a day (photo: Pat Scala).

The working animals

A mere seven horses arrived with the First Fleet but by the latter half of the 19th century, Australia was envied around the world for the fact that just about everybody could afford a horse. Australia also became famous for the prowess and bravery of its riders. They were known for their capacity to gallop at speed down steep inclines—an image promoted by the writers and painters of the day. First the stockmen, then the Australian Light Horse in the Boer War and the Great War became heroes on horseback. Out on the cattle and sheep stations being able to handle a horse was fundamental to the job, and managing a difficult one, a badge of honour. But in those early days equipment was often rudimentary and horse nutrition unheard of. This meant the average stockman or drover needed almost twice as many horses as are needed today to travel the distance and do the job. The early settlers soon realised that the European saddles they brought with them couldn't take the rough terrain—and more often than not, the rougher horses and riders. Saddlers in the 1860s started to experiment with stronger saddle trees, deeper seats and high pommels and the Australian Stock saddle was born.

Bullock drays were the mainstay of farming families, explorers and miners when it came to moving heavy loads. Bullocks bred in Australia were a mixture of English and Bos Indicus types. Their early importation was questioned by bureaucrats back in England as an extravagance, but by the 1820s bullock teams had become the preferred method of hauling. They were the most cost-effective land transport. A bullock team and dray cost about the same as a modern truck would today. The teams remained in work well into the railway age, and they continued to work in the timber industry, wherever the terrain was difficult, until well into the 1960s.

Although early settlers made many mistakes, they were on to a good thing with camels. Cobb & Co. used them instead of horses on their Wilcannia to Mount Browne route during the droughts of the 1880s. Then, with the prospect of desert fighting—and ideal training conditions at home—the Australian Army made up a significant part of the Imperial Camel Corps in World War I (pictured here is the Army Camel Corp. in training at Menangle Park, in 1916). And camels are still very much in evidence today, farmed for their meat, exported to the Middle East or employed to give tourists rides through the outback. **Overleaf:** for many years, genuine horsepower was the vital driving force on the farm (photos: H.H. Fishwick).

Despite technology's advances, horses are still valuable in droving, where they are thought to cause less stress to animals than motorised vehicles—and they are undeniably more romantic. Bruce McCormack with son Adam at Craig's Hut, in 2005, where *The Man From Snowy River* was filmed in the 1980s. The family has been grazing cattle in the high country since the beginning of the 19th century; the government has now banned grazing in the area (photo: Simon O'Dwyer).

Industrious, clever and loyal, working dogs are invaluable to the Australian farmer. So popular are his kelpies that breeder Ian O'Connell **(opposite top)** contributes to the annual Casterton Working Dog Auction, which he helped to found (photo: Simon Schluter). Quality working dogs **(opposite bottom)** such as Custard, right, his son Grub, rear, and another of his pups are in high demand (photo: Peter Stoop). A four-legged contender shows off his talents **(opposite left)** during sheepdog trials (photo: Greg Newington). At the end of a hard day **(above)**, dogs are a farmer's true blue companion (photo: Joe Armao).

The new ventures

The bush has entered a new phase of development with farmers venturing into new crops, going organic and even re-inventing themselves as accommodation operators. More than 1.5 million people a year visit a farm for their holidays—with about 350,000 of them coming from overseas.

Side-by-side with tourism is a burgeoning regional food and wine industry. Australia is now one of the world's major wine producers exporting to more than 80 countries. There are grape producers in every state and territory and 60 defined wine-growing regions, reflecting a big range of climates and soil types.

The foodie tourist can fossick around local producers and farmers' gate sales in search of anything from home-produced cheeses, ice-creams, olives and sauces, to fruits, herbs and spices. Country towns hold popular farmers' markets and delis are springing up in the high streets. Smart young chefs are leaving the cities and setting up award-winning restaurants in the country. The trend towards fresh is also underpinning Australia's fast-expanding organics industry. With more hectares devoted to this type of production than any other country in the world, Australia is producing organic tea, coffee, wheat and beef as well as fruit and vegetables.

Road trips haven't changed much **(above)**; an H.H. Fishwick image of a car travelling the great Princes Highway, near Tilba Tilba, in 1934. The famous Morpeth Sourdough Bakery **(opposite)** in the Hunter Valley has family connections with the Arnott's Biscuits empire; Stephen and Allison Arnott, pictured with three-year-old Mackenzie in October 2006, are the owners of this successful business which supplies bread to hundreds of retail outlets throughout NSW and encourages tourist visitation (photo: Simone De Peak).

It's not just hard yakka. The bush has become a gourmand's paradise: the Lindemans winery at Pokolbin, NSW **(above)**, attracts wine-lovers and foodies alike (photo: Glen McCurtayne). In Moyne Shire, Victoria, a guide **(opposite bottom)** explains native flora to visitors from Yangzhou, China (photo: Damian White). And those who like to see the country in style can sit back and watch it fly by from the airconditioned comfort of The Ghan **(opposite bottom)**; the trip from Adelaide to Darwin takes 53 hours (photo: Glen Campbell).

THE GHAN
AN3

THE

THE PEOPLE

When James Cook was preparing the former coal ship *The Endeavour* in 1765 to sail for Tahiti to observe the Transit of Venus, and then to follow clandestine orders to search for Van Diemen's Land and New Holland, there were an estimated 300,000 Aborigines living across what is now Australia.

In 1788, Captain Arthur Phillip added to the mix, bringing 1030 convicts, marines and sailors—plus one bull, one bull calf, four cows, and a few sheep, horses and goats. By 1858, the white population had reached one million.

By Federation there were 3.8 million whites and an estimated 94,500 Aborigines. Almost half the white population lived on rural properties or in small towns. In stark contrast, by the end of the 20th century less than 18 per cent of Australians—including Aborigines—lived in the bush and many of the city and suburban dwellers rarely, if ever, travelled beyond the slim strip of the coastal population belt.

It has often been said that there are two Australias existing side by side—urban Australia and the bush. This has never been truer. And with each passing year the gap widens. Back in the city we can only admire our rural counterparts for their spirit and resilience in the face of extraordinary difficulties, usually caused by either one or both of two key factors: climate and distance.
On a daily basis, they deal cheerfully and capably with events that would have a city dweller rushing for a triple 0 call. The people of the bush are invariably unpretentious and unassuming. Yet despite of—perhaps because of—the hardships of life there is an energy and fortitude about them that is both humbling and inspiring.

The Aborigines

Indigenous Australians represent our past, present and future. Prior to European settlement, their population is thought to have numbered up to one million, but the turbulent times that followed devastated their diverse tribes. From widespread decimation by the early settlers to the ongoing sadnesses of the Stolen Generation, there is much to regret. Although their culture has been treated with more sensitivity and respect in recent times, there is much work to be done. The irony is, of course, that for generations of European bush residents, the Aborigines have been a source of invaluable wisdom and assistance in what is otherwise a harsh, unforgiving environment.

Aboriginal elder, Jacob Puntaru **(above)**, throws a spear using a woomera on the Liru walk, near Uluru (photo: Quentin Jones). A native woman and child **(opposite)** at Tarcoola station on the Trans Australia Railway Route.

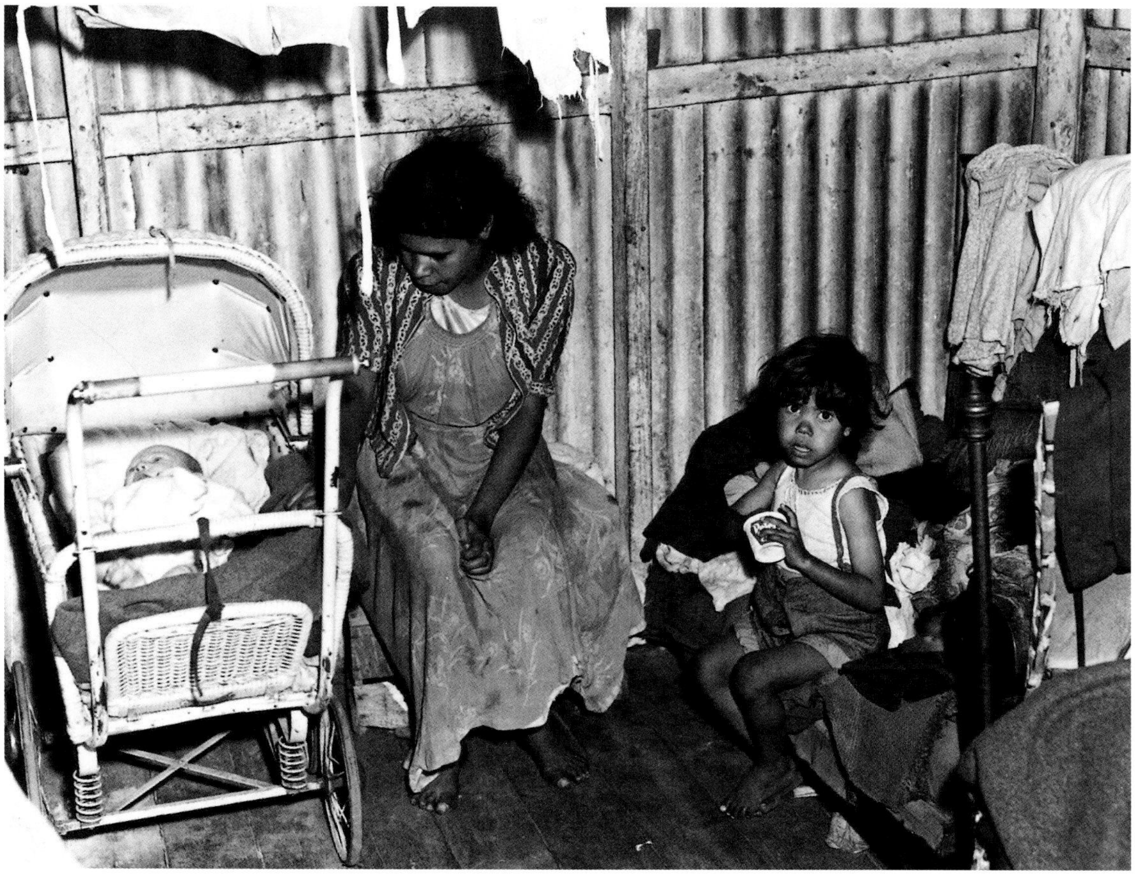

Official attitudes to Aborigines have varied widely; this group of prisoners **(opposite top)** in 1960s Alice Springs was forced to work harnessed to a cart, guarded by a policeman with a loaded rifle. In contrast, police have long respected the supreme skills of native trackers such as Arthur Koosnoy **(opposite bottom)**, who helped in the search for Steven Walls at Guyra in 1960 (photo: Bob Rice). Many Aboriginal families lived in cramped conditions on settlements, such as this one pictured in December 1951 **(above)**.

In this arresting 1924 photo by H.H. Fishwick **(above)**, an Aboriginal woman dances for passengers travelling on the Trans Australia Railway Route in South Australia; an Aboriginal woman poses with a child **(opposite)** for an unknown photographer at Tarcoola station.

Many Aboriginal people today are successfully using Western knowledge to help their own and other communities. Jane Williams **(right)**, pictured running the eye clinic for the Bourke Aboriginal Health Service in December 2004 (photo: Anthony Johnson).

Between 1915 and 1969 the children of the Stolen Generation, who were often of mixed descent, were taken to missions such as this one at Mulgoa, NSW, photographed in 1948 **(opposite top)**. Although it was thought that the children would benefit from better health and education, the *Bringing Them Home* report (published in 1997), shows the effect was devastating on the children and their families; the racial divide still casts a shadow over the younger generation. These young boys **(opposite bottom)** were pictured in Bourke in February 1997 (photo: Palani Mohan).

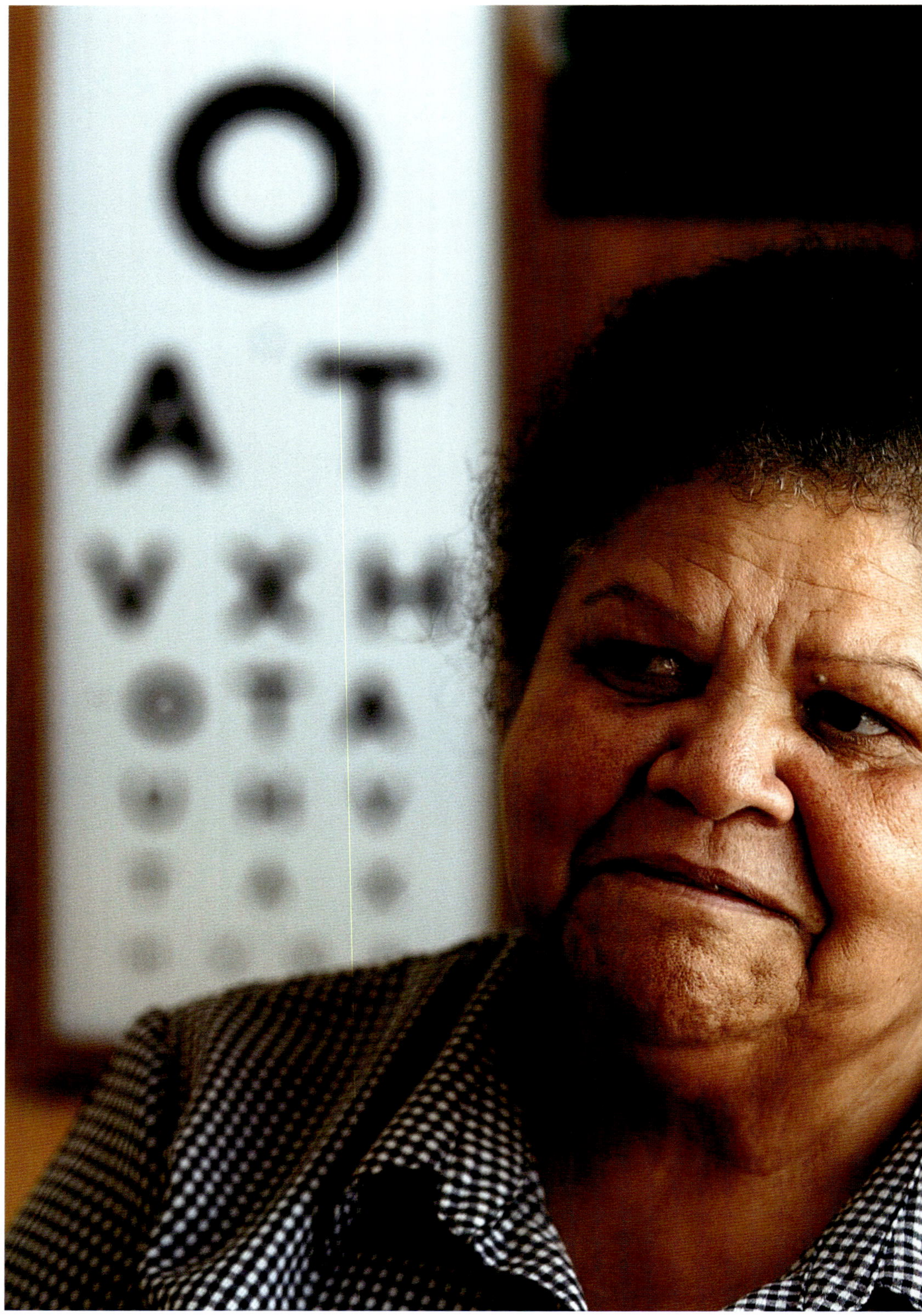

The women

Too often the silent partner in the business of the bush, women have in fact played a starring role as the backbone of outback life: raising families, running homesteads, managing stations—not to mention injecting a sense of style and compassion into a tough environment. Their spirit, endurance and resourcefulness resulted in the creation of the community groups such as the Country Women's Association, and greatly assisted with the continued running of farms during the world wars. Their bush story is an important one to tell.

The contrasts of women's bush work . . . Living on the Yanco property with her family in 1988 Rose Cameron **(above)** would visit Jerilderie once a week, Wagga Wagga once a month and Sydney or Melbourne a few times a year to stave off isolation (photo: John Nobley). Farmer Lu Hogan **(opposite far left)** drives the tractor with her three-year-old son next to her (photo: Craig Sillitoe). Michelle Scott competes in the 2005 women's breakaway roping **(opposite left)** at the Gresford Rodeo, NSW (photo: Stefan Moore).

During World War II, women filled gaps in the rural workforce. On camps such as this one in June 1940 at Gundagai, NSW **(above right)**, they learned how to operate machinery and handle livestock (photo: G. Short). And, as far back as the early part of the 20th century, women worked in the mining industry **(above)**, living in primitive conditions in order to pan for gold. It wasn't all work, however: there was the 1954 Royal Easter Show to attend **(top)** and pea-picking championships to compete in **(opposite)**, such as this one at Port Macquarie in October 1943 (photo: Harry Martin).

Today, of course, women participate in all aspects of working life. Three members of the Department of Natural Resources and Environment **(left)** were also volunteer firefighters, in March 2000 (photo: Matthew Bouwmeester). Maureen Muggeridge **(above right)** was very much aware of being a woman in a man's world, but it didn't stop her from mining in December 2006 (photo: Megan Lewis). And Lisa Hansch **(above left)** graduated from shearing school in Tasmania in 2005 as only the second female shearer in the state (photo: John Woudstra). The traditional roles for women were very much in evidence in the 1960s; here, farmers' wives make tea at Guyra while the menfolk search for Steven Walls, the Little Boy Lost **(opposite)**.

PUBLIC SCHOOL
1898

The children

The bush child is a symbol of hope and renewal in a world where so little is constant. Photographic images of children at outback schools, playing in the scrub or helping out on the farm are plentiful, as are artists' dedications to the Australian bush youth in the form of paintings, verse and books such as the May Gibbs classic *Snugglepot and Cuddlepie*. Although it can no longer be taken for granted that a farmer's child will take over the family business, there can be no doubt that the energy and vitality of bush youth continues to drive the country community.

Children living close enough to town have long enjoyed the intimate education available at the country school. A physical training class was often on the agenda, seen here in 1912 at Failford public school near Nabiac, NSW **(opposite)**. Small class numbers create new challenges for today's schools **(above)**, such as at Benambra, Victoria, in 2000, where the entire school population consists of 14 kids and the teacher (photo: Jason South).

For those on more isolated properties, education might mean heading off to boarding school in the city, such as these children from Cashmere Station near Caragabal, NSW, in 1942 **(opposite)**. Alternatively, there's the School of the Air **(above left)**, which opened in 1951; the students pictured are based on a settlement in Alice Springs, in 1962. Whereas lessons in 1997 **(above right)** don't look all that different from previous decades, more and more students are now benefitting from interactive technology, such as the internet, DVDs, CDs and satellite communication (photo: Sandy Scheltema).

Growing up in the bush provides plenty of opportunity for play. Joining dad **(above left)** as he does the rounds feeding the sheep at Hillview Farm near Cootamundra, NSW, in May 1951 (photo: Frank Burke). The Bourke Olympic Pool **(above right)** is a focus for fun and games (photo: Andrew Meares). Using a 44-gallon drum, 16-year-old professional bull rider Shea Fisher **(opposite)** practises for the Mt Isa rodeo (photo: Brendan Esposito). Getting together at a youth centre in Bourke **(opposite far right)**, where kids are provided with activities to beat boredom (photo: Palani Mohan).

YOUTH

The migrants

Of course, the first settlers can be termed 'migrants', but those adventurous souls who arrived in this country in later centuries have also played a huge part in the development of Australia. Whether they arrived from Poland to help build power stations or from China during the gold rush, their mark is evident in all aspects of bush life: the architecture, the food, the politics, the religion and the slang. Searching for an easier life for themselves and their families, they encountered all manner of new worries, but it's an understatement to say they helped shape the nation.

For recent immigrants, life in a new country brought constant discoveries. In 1956 Dutch housewife Mrs Mia Dolega Jasienska **(above left)** found that her washing was as likely to freeze as dry on Mount Kosciuszko. Others chanced upon love, such as this gypsy couple **(above right)** getting married in 1937 (photo: Kimbel). British migrants in 1951 **(opposite bottom)** adapted to basic living conditions at the migrant centre in Bathurst (photo: Bertram Jones). The only known picture of Beechworth's Chinatown before it was destroyed by fire early in the 20th century **(opposite top)**.

Being so far from home made it easy to forge new friendships. A French-Canadian, an Irishman, two Maltese, an Italian and an Australian share lunch **(opposite top)** while working on the Snowy Mountains Hydro-Electric Scheme, built between 1949 and 1974. Polish immigrants play cards at Tarraleah, Tasmania, in 1947 **(opposite bottom)**.

The influx of Chinese migrants was to forever alter Australia's culture. Chinese migrants from Hong Kong being off-loaded into the surf at Cooktown, Queensland, in 1875 **(above right)**; attracted by gold discoveries, they became 'human cargo' in ships returning from the Far East. Chinese Miners in Walhalla District, Victoria, about 1904 **(above left)**.

Losing your way is all too easy in the bush. These three lucky hikers **(above)** got caught in a bushfire but found shelter in a mountain stream; they returned safely from the Baw Baws, Victoria, in 1930 just before searchers set out. In February 1960, 3500 people helped to find the Little Boy Lost, Steven Walls **(opposite)**, when he went missing for 77 hours near Guyra, NSW (photo: Bob Rice).

The mysteries

For all its baking sunshine and wide open spaces, there is an eeriness that hangs about the Australian bush, particularly for those not living in it. This dark side compels and repels us. The missing child is a continuing theme —depicted most famously in Frederick McCubbin's oil painting of 1886, *Lost*— as is the Australian version of Grimms' fairy tales, in the form of the haunting Aboriginal dreamtime stories. Then there are the notorious, and often unsolved, murders. The intriguing Pyjama Girl mystery and the tragic Azaria Chamberlain case are just two of the more infamous.

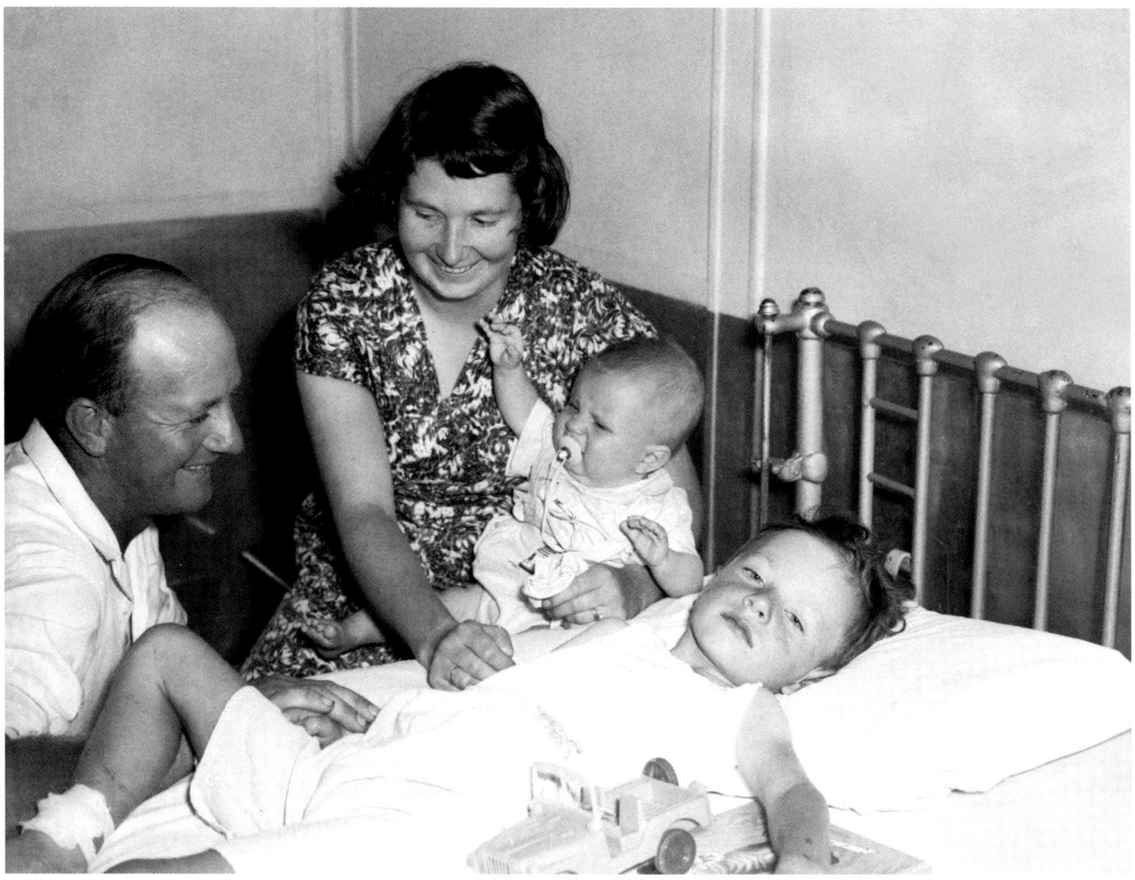

The seemingly unsolvable crimes . . . In 1934 the body of a woman was discovered in a culvert under a road near Albury, NSW, sparking one of Australia's most famous mysteries; with no means of identifying her, she became known as the Pyjama Girl for the luxury silk clothing she had been wearing when she was shot or beaten to death **(above)**. Ten years later police identified her as English party girl Linda Agostini, but recent research suggests this was wrong.

In the early 1980s Lindy Chamberlain's claim that a dingo had taken her baby at Uluru captured public attention; she leads a camera crew through bush in August 1982 **(opposite top)**. She and her husband Michael appealed to the press **(opposite bottom)** on the steps of the Alice Springs courthouse in February 1981, after the first inquest into Azaria's death (photo: Russell McPhedran). Lindy was convicted of her daughter's murder in 1982. This was overturned in 1988 when new evidence cleared her name.

The political scene

Once upon a time, the greatest challenges in bush residents were the weather and the vast distances. Now, political problems are just as trying for country folk. Aboriginal land rights, conservation, dying towns and rivers, financial assistance for farmers . . . the list is certainly lengthy and the issues by no means close to resolution. Whatever the reigning political party, however, the bush community has always looked after its own—the generations of soldiers sent off to war being a fine example—and has continued to have a soft spot for royalty, in the face of city-based republicanism.

The Father of Federation, Sir Henry Parkes **(opposite)** vocalised his impassioned support for Federation with his famous 'oration' at the School of Arts in Tenterfield, NSW, in 1889. The call to fight in World War II was bravely met by men of the country, but in these small communities, such as Hay in NSW, their loss was keenly felt **(above top)**. In 1954 Queen Elizabeth became the first reigning monarch to tour Australia **(above)**. On a visit to a country fair in Dubbo she was greeted with an honour guard of 100 stud sheep—or, at least, their rear ends.

DOWN WITH THE CHINESE

Many of the political principles that guided Australia were cast in the heady atmosphere of the goldfields. Joyce Simpson **(above)**, president of the Young Historical Society Lambing Flat Museum in November 2006, pictured with the 'Roll Up' flag, the third most important flag in Australia's history (photo: Kate Geraghty). The flag, with 'No Chinese' painted on it, was used in the Lambing Flat riots; over nine months in 1860 and 1861, 3000 gold-hungry men turned on the Chinese miners **(opposite)**. A Miners' Protective League sought the expulsion of Chinese, repeal of gold duties and parliamentary representation.

Long before the Mabo ruling of 1992, Aboriginal land rights were at the forefront of bush politics. In early 1985 protestors **(opposite)** marched for six days from Alice Springs to Canberra trying to secure native titles (photo: Lorrie Graham). Later that same year the Governor-General Sir Ninian Stephen performed a handover ceremony for Ayers Rock **(above)**, now Uluru.

LAND OWNS
US
BUT WE
BLACK
SOVEREIGN
PEOPLE

Protests come in many forms. An anti-logging demcnstration **(opposite)** in Chaelundi State Forest, NSW, in July 1991 led to turbulent scenes (photo: Rick Stevens). The bush against Bush: 250 men stripped naked **(above top)** to comment on the 'small man syndrome that leads to the need for big guns' in February 2003 (photo: Heath Missen). Of course, the conventional way of making your voice heard is by casting your vote **(above)**, seen here in the remote area of Narriearra, near Tibooburra, NSW (photo: Steven Siewert).

STAWELL ATHLETIC CLUB.

The events

Laughing in the face of adversity is a bush trait. And nothing embodies unfailing optimism quite like a game of outback cricket, a boozy B&S ball, a country show or a quirky contest. Teamwork, mateship, competition, victory and loss are all things that are experienced daily in the bush, and the lighthearted practicing of them in the form of community events is a welcome respite from hard work and unpredictable lifestyles.

Certain bush events are followed by sport-lovers nationwide. The Silver City Cup in Broken Hill brings everyone together for a drink, a bit of a flutter and an all-round good time **(above)**. The 1950 winner of the classic Stawell Gift **(opposite)**; the original of the 120-metre race was run in 1878 as a bit of fun for gold rush miners.

International Rodeo Stampede

Bush sports so often involve man and beast. A photo of a farmer and his dog hunting in northern Queensland in 1929 by H.H. Fishwick **(opposite left)**. Roughrider Joe Johnston tackles a lively steer at the Moomba Rodeo and Stampede in 1955, the first year of the parade **(opposite top)**. The Murray Valley Hunt Club in 1956 ready themselves for a traditional fox hunt at Wilberforce, NSW **(opposite below)**.

Maybe it's the sun, maybe it's the isolation, but the bush certainly has some weird and wonderful festivals. Elvis is alive and well in Parkes, NSW, which celebrates the King every January **(above)**. Camel racing **(above left)** is the name of the game at the Blackall races, in western Queensland (photo: Sean Davey). And, it started as a joke, but now up to 50 or more competitors battle the 800-metre creek swim **(left)**, the 20-kilometre bike ride and the five laps of the town in the Dirt & Dust Triathlon of Julia Creek, Queensland (photo: Andy Zakeli).

They're a rite of passage and a rollicking good time. After the Governor had left, the party-goers relaxed at the debutante ball in Broken Hill **(above top)**. How to down your drink **(above)** at the Stone Rollers Bachelors and Spinsters Ball at Murray Bridge, South Australia (photo: Craig Sillitoe).

Where would country Australia be without its shows? Ken Connley **(left)** wins the Cattlemen's Cup in Omeo, Victoria, in 1985. Champion pumpkin growers Keith and Colin Dixon **(above left)** at their Nepean Park farm in December 1997; the vegetables were to be supplied for the Western Districts display at the Royal Easter Show (photo: Robert Pearce). Woodchopping is always a crowd-pleaser **(above)**; Dennis Hines of Nowra powers his way through the upright event at the Albion Park Show, NSW, in 2001 (photo: Andy Zakeli).

THE
SPI

RIT

THE SPIRIT

The bush has always played a big part in the way Australians see themselves. It started way back in the early days when the country life was romantically projected to new settlers as the antidote to a rapidly industrialising Britain.

Bush people were portrayed as having simple, decent values that exemplified the best national characteristics—such as mateship, egalitarianism, irreverence and stoicism.

The stockman was a hero on horseback; the drover enviably free from the shackles of life; the bushranger a daring rebel, and a symbol of resistance against authority. Yet, most of the writers and painters who sustained the mythology were delivering their message from the safety of the city. Henry Lawson, A.B. 'Banjo' Paterson, Sir Arthur Streeton and Tom Roberts and were all living and working in cities.

Famously, it sparked *The Bulletin* debate which saw Lawson and Paterson slug it out on the pages of the national magazine. Lawson accused Paterson of over-romanticising the Bush and Paterson countered by claiming—in verse, of course—that Lawson was far too depressing.

The bush has been inspiring poets and painters, novelists and filmmakers, singers and even politicians, ever since. In the seemingly never ending search for a national identity, the bush has been pored over, pilloried, despised and dignified. It has given us many of our heroes, both real and fictional: Ned Kelly, Burke and Wills, 'The Man From Snowy River', *Crocodile Dundee*, even Phar Lap. It was, perhaps, the boys who emptied the small country towns during World War I who we remember best.

Despite our increasingly urbanised lives, and the demographic changes that are making us more multicultural and outward looking, after more than 200 years of rumination, the bush will unquestionably continue to be central to our attempts to make sense of the forces that have shaped us, what it is to be Australian, and the development of our national self image.

"You feel free in Australia. There is great relief in the atmosphere—a relief from tension, from pressure, an absence of control of will or form. The skies open above you and the areas open around you."

D.H. Lawrence

The Sydney Morning Herald had its own DC3, which it used to fly newspapers to remote areas **(above)**. George Bell **(opposite)** captured the true pioneering spirit of early bush settlers; he started with *The Sydney Morning Herald* in 1908 as the newspaper's first full-time photographer. The portrait was taken by Herbert Fishwick, a fellow recorder of bush life, while the image of Bell on his horse in 1910 shows his cumbersome equipment, a bulky Ross twin-lens reflex camera.

The news

The intrepid nature of those who live and work in the bush has long been captured by equally intrepid Australian journalists; in the early years of the 20th century by legendary photographers H.H. Fishwick and George Bell and reporter Charles Bean, through to the present day coverage in newspapers and magazines, on TV and radio. It provides a valuable record of what life is really like in the outback, as well as enabling the passage of information between remote communities, and the bridging of the gap between country dwellers and those in the cities.

Newspapers—along with magazines, radio, TV and the internet—are an invaluable way for people in remote areas to keep in touch with the news, and for the rest of Australia to understand the issues that concern the bush. The Australian bush and its residents have long made the front page of national papers **(opposite)** such as the bushfire coverage in *The Age*, January 15, 1962, and their supplements **(above)**—here, the *Good Weekend* edition of August 14, 2004 (photo: Marco Del Grande).

FORECAST: City: Still Dry and Warm. Highest Temperature Near Ninety.

Classified Index Page 10

The Age

POSTAL ADDRESS: 233 COLLINS STREET, C.1. TELEPHONES: 63 0341; CLASSIFIED ADVERTISING: 63 0301

No. 33,289 [Registered at G.P.O., Melbourne, for Transmission by Post as a Newspaper] MELBOURNE, MONDAY, JANUARY 15, 1962 16 PAGES PRICE 4d.

Shadow of Destruction on Ranges

STATE'S WORST BUSH FIRES SINCE 1939 STRIKE THE DANDENONGS

23 Homes Destroyed; Sanctuary Menaced

VICTORIA'S worst bush fires since 1939 ravaged the ranges east of Melbourne yesterday.

At least 23 homes were burnt to the ground and flames swept part of the Sir Colin Mackenzie wild life sanctuary at Healesville.

Today has been declared a day of acute fire danger throughout the State. No fires may be lit in the open anywhere in Victoria.

More than 2000 fire fighters battled against searing flames and choking smoke to control fires in the Dandenongs.

"Whole mountains seemed to be on fire," said a man who flew over the area in a plane.

Thousands of acres of bush were destroyed by the galloping flames.

No deaths were reported, but many people had narrow escapes.

At least three fire fighters were bitten by snakes.

Century-plus temperatures and tinder dry conditions after Victoria's long dry spell helped the fires take hold.

Worst outbreak was in the Sassafras-Olinda district in the Dandenongs, where 18 houses were destroyed.

A heavy pall of white smoke over the Dandenongs shut out the blistering January sun from the ground.

The smoke clouds, pushing hundreds of feet into the air, could be seen from many Melbourne suburbs.

Late last night the fire was still burning. Scores of people living near The Basin were standing by to evacuate their homes.

In the Healesville blaze, three houses, a timber mill and a fire truck were destroyed.

Others fires which flared throughout Victoria yesterday were:

- **CHRISTMAS HILLS-YARRA GLEN.** One fire was soon under control but the other swept towards Yarra Glen, threatening the township, and was still burning last night. Two houses were destroyed.
- **LANCEFIELD.** A fire, believed to have been started by young boys smoking out a ferret, burnt 250 acres of bush at the foot of Mt. William.
- **BADGER CREEK.** — One fire, which threatened an army camp, was brought under control. A second fire swept along the Yarra Valley and last night was still raging.
- **CLEAR LAKE-DOUGLAS.**—A scrub fire reported here, 35 miles south-west of Horsham, was still burning late yesterday.
- **APSLEY.**—More than 350 acres of land were burnt in this fire on the South Australian border.

Other fires were reported at Ringwood, Heathmont, Rosebud and Coldstream.

The Dandenongs fire started at The Basin late yesterday morning.

By late last night it had burned through to Olinda, threatening Sassafras on the way, and returned to within two miles of The Basin.

Thousands of people with homes in the area packed their cars with clothing and were ready to flee to safety.

The operations manager of Nicholas Air Charter Pty. Ltd. (Mr. R. Cavill) told a dramatic story after flying over the Dandenongs.

"It was a terrifying experience," he said. "Whole mountains seemed to be on fire.

"We could hear explosions as houses went up in a whoosh!

"Around Mount Dandenong it was as though a whole city were on fire."

Hundreds of sightseers, attracted by radio news broadcasts, seriously hampered firefighters.

Many had to be turned back toward Melbourne by cruising police courtesy cars.

Ten police cars from Melbourne, every policeman in the district, all fire brigades in a 40-mile radius, ambulanes and busloads of volunteers crowded the narrow, winding roads.

The Country Fire Authority yesterday rushed extra rural tanker trucks and equipment from as far as Ballarat, Bendigo and Morwell to help fight the fires in the hills around Melbourne.

The assistant chief fire officer (Mr. C. H. Howe) said more equipment would be brought today from Mildura and other north - western centres, where the fire danger was not so critical.

At Healesville on Saturday a fire brigade captain was killed and four fire fighters injured when their fire truck overturned racing to a fire.

●Continued on Page 3.

TV Tower in Danger

Early this morning the Dandenongs fire was threatening the transmitters of Melbourne's three television stations at Mt. Dandenong.

Destruction of the transmitters would put the channels off the air.

"We are not panic-stricken, but there is a possibility our transmitter will go," a GTV-9 spokesman said at 1 a.m.

The transmitters were threatened earlier in the day, but a change in the wind saved them.

STOP PRESS

Plane Missing in Arid Bight Region

ADELAIDE, Sunday. — A single-engined light aircraft was eight hours overdue at Cook, in the wild far west of South Australia, late tonight.

The plane, a Wackett, took off on the 200-mile flight from Ceduna at 12.15 p.m. today with only the pilot aboard. The pilot's name has not been released.

Acute Fire Danger Today

Century Heat in City —Then Slump

Melbourne's temperature soared to the century mark yesterday for the second time this summer—then slumped 12 degrees in five minutes as a cool sea breeze replaced searing northerlies.

This is how the temperature rose in Melbourne yesterday.

Time	Temp. (deg.)	Hum. (p.c.)
5.30 a.m. (min.)	56	—
6 a.m.	68	76
7 a.m.	66	—
8 a.m.	75	—
9 a.m.	89.1	22
10 a.m.	94	—
11 a.m.	96	—
Noon	95.4	17
1 p.m.	98	—
1.20 p.m. (max.)	100	—
2 p.m.	84	—
3 p.m.	81	48
4 p.m.	80	—
5 p.m.	79	—
6 p.m.	77.2	48
7 p.m.	76	—
8 p.m.	74	—
9 p.m.	71.6	65

37 Saved in Three Sea Rescues

A total of 37 people were saved in three dramatic mass rescues from Victorian beaches yesterday.

At Brighton Beach 16 people—mostly children—were saved after they got into difficulties at a small beach between the baths and a groyne jutting 20 yards into the sea.

At Parkdale five life savers, including two girls, rescued 11 people from drowning in choppy seas.

At Sorrento 10 swimmers were rescued by surf patrols in a hectic mass rescue during a surf carnival yesterday morning.

A crowd of nearly 10,000 saw the rescues.

. . . And two naval ratings were rescued off Cowes on Saturday afternoon, after a policeman commissioned the local ferry.

See Page 5.

● SUFFOCATING CLOUDS OF SMOKE rise hundreds of feet into the sky over the Dandenongs yesterday. TOP: As the fire spread from The Basin to Sassafras, the smoke cast a long shadow from its path of destruction across the trees to Boronia. LOWER: This was the scene from a plane 1300 feet up as the fire reached the outskirts of Sassafras yesterday afternoon.

In Other Pages

NEWS:

FEATURES:

SERVICES:

Classified Advertisements Index Page 10

The artists

Regardless of whether you hail from the bush or not, there is something undeniably moving about Frederick McCubbin's 1904 oil triptych *The Pioneer*, Peter Weir's 1975 film *Picnic at Hanging Rock*, or Dorothea Mackellar's 1908 poem 'My Country'. Since the time of the first settlers, the Australian bush—whether it be the red deserts, fragrant eucalypts, colourful outback characters or the Aboriginal dreamtime—has inspired artists of all persuasions: writers, painters, filmmakers and poets. Today, there is a fiercely competitive (and controversial) market for Aboriginal artworks that illustrates exactly how coveted an artist's representation of bush ambiance can be.

Artists find an inexhaustible supply of inspiration in the wildness and beauty of the bush and in man's struggle to survive. Esteemed Aboriginal artist Albert Namatjira, in September 1958, depicting the ancient splendour of the Arrernte lands around Alice Springs **(opposite)**. Artist Marion Borgelt designed the interactive Round Up Maze in 2005 **(above)** for the Shear Outback Museum, Hay, in collaboration with Andrew Crick, after seeing Peter Leaver's iconic aerial photograph of 2000 sheep (photo: Kate Geraghty).

The outback poets have given us some of our most enduring images of rural life. Henry Lawson **(above)** was born on the goldfields of Grenfell, NSW, in 1867 and, although his later life took him to Sydney, his stories conveyed the loneliness, hardship, mateship and humour that we now all associate with the bush (photo: State Library of NSW). A.B. 'Banjo' Paterson **(left)** enjoyed a rivalry with Lawson; a series of verses were published where they debated their different perspectives on the Australian bush—Lawson claiming Paterson was a romantic, and Paterson claiming Lawson was full of doom and gloom. H.H. Fishwick's 1933 photo taken at the top of Jacob's Ladder **(opposite top)**, looking down on the Snowy River, could come straight from Banjo Paterson's iconic poem. Bush legend Campbell the Swaggie **(opposite bottom)**, pictured at the 125th anniversary of the siege of Glenrowan in 2005, delivers bush poetry throughout the country (photo: Craig Sillitoe).

KATE KELLY'S
Souvenirs
NED KELLY

The symbols

Some things instantly transport the city dweller to the bush, or the Aussie expat back to his homeland. The billy can, the gum tree, the pub, the outback dunny, the beer ad, the ute . . . There are many more iconic images of the bush, but these six in particular have a hold over our senses.

Ask anyone to visualise the bush, and somewhere in that image there will be a gum tree. A four-year-old boy **(opposite far left)** is dwarfed by a thick forest of 300-year-old blue gums, in July 1995 (photo: Brendan Esposito); H.H. Fishwick's stunning early image of paperbark trees in Western Australia **(opposite)**; a conservationist **(above)** collects the seeds of River Red Gums by the Little Murray River (photo: Ray Kennedy); the Aussie version of the Christmas tree **(above right)** in Mooroopna, Victoria (photo: Pat Scala).

Previous page: old man river—a moment of reflection under a great gum in 1910 by George Bell; and a true bushman never travels without his billy—on the Gresford Cattle Drive in 2006, bacon, snags and billy tea are an essential start to the day (photo: Kitty Hill).

At the end of a hard day, there's nothing better than exchanging a few yarns over a cold one. The country pub, such as the Bulli Family Hotel **(above)**, NSW, pictured in 1974, is at the heart of every town, while its locals are a town's lifeblood. While cars need fuel, men need beer **(opposite top)**, and bush hotels have no shortage of signs to tempt the tastebuds; these stockmen from Anna Creek station enjoy a cold one at the William Creek pub in April 2000 (photo: Steven Siewert). Not all is as it seems at this outback 'pub' near Broken Hill in May 1997 **(opposite bottom)**; there is nothing behind the façade of corrugated iron and timber, but it's recognisable as the outback setting of numerous XXXX beer ads (photo: Sahlan Hayes).

•ICE COLD BEERS
•PETROL, DIESEL
•TYRE REPAIRS
VB
GATEWAY TO
DESERT & LA

Holden introduced the ute in 1951, and it's now an Aussie icon, a symbol of hard work and a laid-back lifestyle. This farmer **(above)** is pictured with his four sons and the family's 1959 Holden ute at Dappo, NSW, in 1995 (photo: Peter Rae); a pub owner **(right)** poses on his ute outside the Cumberland Hotel, Smeaton, in June 2001 (photo: Simon O'Dwyer). Sometimes you just need a bit of peace and quiet, and where better than the dunny **(opposite)**, that symbol of bush practicality and simplicity (photo: Louie Douvis)?

The music

From the traditional indigenous didgeridoo, to bush ballads, to the explosion of Country & Western, music is central to the outback lifestyle. It also plays the important role of keeper, preserver and promoter of bush myths and history. Straight-talking poetry accompanied by stirring melody is the hallmark of bush music, and those with the gift—such as Slim Dusty, Lee Kernaghan, Yothu Yindi and Midnight Oil—quickly take their place in people's hearts. Whether the song proudly recognises pubs with no beer, wild colonial boys or Aboriginal treaties, there is nothing quite so immediately evocative as bush music.

The eclectic sounds of the Australian bush. Slim Dusty, the bush balladeer who made famous 'The Pub With No Beer', relaxes with a cold can at his local in the 1970s **(opposite)**. One of the country's most revered singer-songwriters, Lee Kernaghan **(top)**, hits the road in true country style (photo: Julian Kingma). Yothu Yindi **(above)**, shown performing at the opening ceremony of the Paralympic Games in Sydney in 2000, mixed traditional Aboriginal sounds with contemporary rock to become Australia's most successful indigenous band; the group's name translates as 'mother and child' (photo: Dallas Kilponen).

JOE MAGUIRE'S PUB
CHAR GRILL
Get well
Slim

Wild Bill Davey **(opposite)**, wearing a 'Get well Slim' T-shirt in January 1999, walks past Joe Maguire's Pub, Tamworth, a key venue for the internationally recognised music festival; Slim Dusty paid homage to the pub with his 1970s song of the same name, and it is apparently where the Tamworth Country Music Festival started (photo: Peter Rae). With all of her solo albums having gone platinum, and with three successive number-one albums on the ARIA charts, Kasey Chambers **(above)**, pictured in December 2006, is always a popular performer (photo: Lisa Wiltse).

Aussie blokes are known for their pragmatic approach to fashion. Not much changes: these miners **(above)**, pictured at Newport in December 1930, wouldn't look out of place today; invented more than 100 years ago by a Scottish sailor who created waterproof coats out of windjammer sails, the hard-wearing Driza-Bone **(opposite)** will never go out of style—and matches perfectly with the trusty Akubra (photo: Ray Kennedy).

The clobber

The harsh bush environment calls for serious gear. Comfort and practicality, not style, reign supreme in the country—but that's not to say that some stellar items haven't gone on to conquer the mainstream fashion world. Think of R.M. Williams clothes and accessories, or the Ugg boot. And, of course, Akubras, Driza-Bones, Blundstones, Hard Yakka and Chesty Bonds are household names across the nation, whether you live in the country or the city.

Not only are they presented to visiting dignitaries, but Akubra hats **(above)** are an everyday icon, worn by the working men and women of the bush; here, they grace the heads of farmers at a drought crisis meeting in Parkes, NSW, in May 2005 (photo: Nick Moir). Drover Adam Wilson **(opposite top)** shows off his mud-splattered Blundstones—'Blunnies'—the signature item of the famous boot company that controversially moved its manufacturing from Hobart to Asia in 2007 (photo: Craig Sillitoe). Time for 'smoko' **(opposite bottom)** at the Stroud Rodeo in September 2000, made all the more comfortable thanks to that farmer's friend, the checked flannelette shirt (photo: Simone De Peake).

The bush family

The ability to pull together in times of crisis is central to the character of the bush. Whether it's a natural disaster affecting many or an individual's need for assistance, there is an unspoken bond between bush folk. Of course, it's not just a tragedy that brings out the best. There is a joyous appreciation for the simple things in life—such as time spent together as a family, supporting social groups with like-minded friends, and appreciating the wonders of the natural environment—that is the true mark of the country community.

What bushfire? Bill Dudley **(above)**, a true Aussie battler, defiantly continues his daily routine in January 1994, despite bushfires having burned his house down (photo: Robert Pearce). Firefighters in 1939 prepare to take on a blaze with the most basic of equipment **(opposite)**.

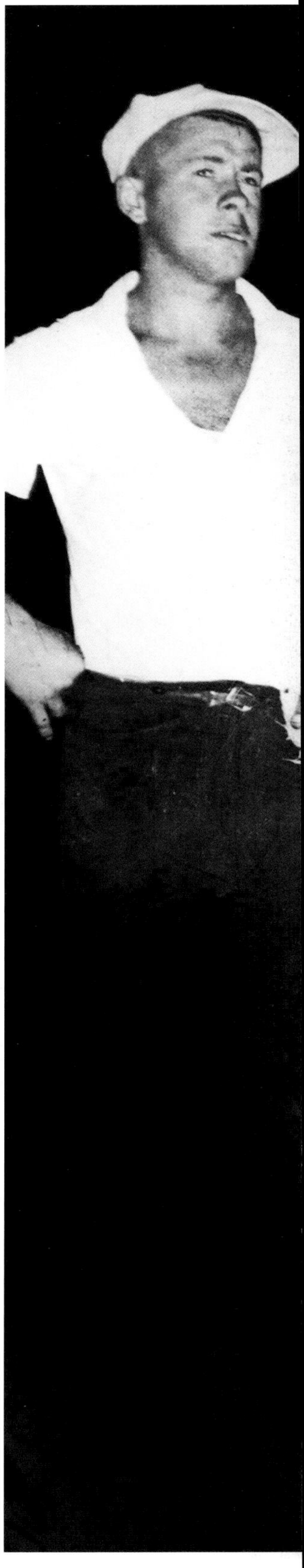

The Country Women's Association **(above)** provides support for women and families in the bush, as well as being an enduring and popular social outlet—members line up at the Aberdeen, NSW, CWA Gymkhana in May 1945. Mrs R. Aldrick **(opposite)**, part of the Teapot Brigade, serves the cuppas at the CWA Ball on the Mornington Peninsula, Victoria, in September 1956.

When the flames threaten, the everyday heroes of the fire services do their utmost to protect property and wildlife; members of the voluntary Illawong Bush Fire Brigade (now the Illawong Rural Fire Service) rest after 14 hours' work at Spencer, NSW, in 1994 **(opposite)**.

Despite the vast distances, the healthcare professionals of the Royal Flying Doctor Service are in close contact with their communities. When the service started in 1928, they used a De Havilland DH50 bi-plane made of cloth and wood; the patients were strapped to the wings **(top left)**. A RFDS plane in 1955 **(top right)**. General surgeon Clement Smith **(above)** checks his plane in May 2000 before flying off to perform his weekly operations in country Victoria (photo: Heath Missen).

There are conventional solutions to drought, and then there are the unconventional. For the women of Ouyen, Victoria **(opposite)**, in January 2003, anything was worth a try, including a naked raindance; they're pictured about to disrobe at a rehearsal (photo: Angela Wylie).

Local pride comes to the fore in the annual Tidy Towns competition **(above)**, with state and nationwide awards for practical environmental initiatives; Don Johns, chairman of the awarded Horsham Tidy Towns committee, does the rounds in 2001 (photo: John Woudstra).

Doing his bit for the community, Phill Higgins **(left)** invests time flying around remote areas to teach children physics (photo: Cathryn Tremain).

An iconic George Bell image from 1910 **(above)**. In March 2006 swagman Lloyd Williams **(opposite)** had little need for company other than his dog Tinker, who was always by his side (photo: Ross Duncan).

The rebels

What better way to sign off than with swagmen and bushrangers, those characters who truly epitomise what it means to be from the bush? Inspiring myths, legends and countless moving ballads, these men rebelled (and continue to rebel) against society's rules, seeking freedom and fortune in the most uncommon ways. It's their larrikin approach to life that captures the adventurous and indomitable Australian spirit.

Although they were criminals, the independence and fighting spirit of bushrangers have always captured our imagination. A portrait of the best-loved of them all, Ned Kelly **(above right)**, photographed at Melbourne Gaol on November 10, 1880, the day before he was hanged (photo: Charles Nettleton). A group of policemen pose proudly with their guns at Glenrowan, site of the Kelly Gang's last stand **(top)**. We even celebrated Kelly as a symbol of the nation **(above)** at the opening ceremony of the 2000 Olympics (photo: Dallas Kilponen).

With the glamour of a true bush legend, bushranger Ben Hall died young in a hail of bullets; this sketch shows him with his gang, attacking the Gundagai coach in December 1864 **(opposite top)**. While others worked for their gold, Dan 'Mad Dog' Morgan **(opposite bottom)** preferred to steal it; the notoriously vicious criminal had a price of £1000 on his head by the time he was shot and killed at Peechelba Station, near Wangaratta, in 1865.

Life on their own terms. In 1933 this old man had lived under a railway bridge at Bayo for more than a year, but with shelter, a ready supply of firewood and a river nearby he wasn't doing too badly for the Depression **(above)**. The Hume Highway near Kilmore, Victoria, under the feet of swagman Bill Marney **(opposite)**.

Random House Australia Pty Ltd
Level 3, 100 Pacific Highway, North Sydney, NSW 2060
www.randomhouse.com.au

Sydney New York Toronto
London Auckland Johannesburg

First published by Random House Australia 2007

National Library of Australia
Cataloguing-in-Publication Entry

Robson, Pamela.

The bush.

ISBN 978 1 74166 593 2 (hbk.).
1. Country life – Australia. 2. Land use, Rural – Australia. 3. Rural-urban relations – Australia.
4. Australia – Rural conditions. I. Austin, Nigel. II. Lewis, Daniel. III. Title.

307.720994

Cover photo: Chris Sattlberger/Getty Images
Cover design and internal concept: Jay Ryves/Future Classic
Internal design: Russell Jeffery/Emigraph Creative
Managing Editor, Fairfax Books: Michael Johnston
Product Manager, Fairfax Books: Sophie Leach
Publishing Manager, Fairfax Books: Stephen Berry
Picture Research, Fairfax Books: Paul McLean
Group General Manager, Fairfax Enterprises: Kevin Stokes
Pre-press: *The Age* Imaging Department, *The Sydney Morning Herald* Imaging Department.
Printed and bound by The Australian Book Connection
10 9 8 7 6 5 4 3 2 1